THE
LITTLE
HISTORY
OF
SUFFOLK

THE
LITTLE
HISTORY
OF
SUFFOLK

SARAH E. DOIG

First published 2018

The History Press
The Mill, Brimscombe Port
Stroud, Gloucestershire, GL5 2QG
www.thehistorypress.co.uk

British Library Cataloguing in Publication Data.
A catalogue record for this book is available from the British Library.

ISBN 978 0 7509 8599 4

Typesetting and origination by The History Press
Printed in Turkey

CONTENTS

ABOUT THE AUTHOR

Although Sarah Doig was born in Hertfordshire, she considers herself a Suffolk girl. When she was a 1-year-old, Sarah moved with her family first to Mildenhall and then to Bury St Edmunds, where she was educated. Leaving Suffolk initially to attend university, Sarah found herself away from the county she considered her home for some twenty-seven years. After having travelled the world during her twenty-year career in the Foreign and Commonwealth Office, Sarah could no longer resist the strong pull back to Suffolk, and finally returned in 2010.

She now works as a freelance local history researcher, writer and speaker. Sarah is the author of *The A-Z of Curious Suffolk*, also published by The History Press.

Sarah's website is www.ancestral-heritage.co.uk.

INTRODUCTION

When I was first asked whether I would consider writing *The Little History of Suffolk*, I almost dismissed it as a challenge too great to take on. How can anyone possibly condense the history of the county, from the dawn of time through to the present day, in one small volume? There are many excellent, academic studies of separate historical periods and aspects of Suffolk, as well as *A History of Suffolk* first published in 1985 by two of the very best local historians the county has been lucky enough to have: David Dymond and Peter Northeast. I then realised that the brief for this book was very different and something I felt able and willing to tackle. Primarily, it is designed to be approachable and readable and, by necessity, to be selective rather than comprehensive. *The Little History of Suffolk* is therefore a book written by an author passionate about the history and heritage of the county for like-minded individuals, regardless of their previous knowledge. My mission is also to enthuse others, for the first time, about the county in which they live or visit. The chronological approach allows the reader to either read the book from cover to cover, to select an era to read or to simply dip in at random. Either way, I hope my selection of what I consider the very best bits of Suffolk history stimulates the mind, and leaves you more informed and interested than you were before picking up the book.

Before I end, and you immerse yourself in *The Little History of Suffolk*, I would like to thank my husband, Mike: a Scotsman who has embraced Suffolk life wholeheartedly. More importantly, Mike has patiently proofread drafts of this book and added his thoughts, for which I am grateful. He has also kept me supplied with coffee, food and alcohol at regular intervals and kept the house running smoothly.

1

EARLY SUFFOLK

IN THE BEGINNING

Half a million years ago, the area we now call Suffolk bore no similarity whatsoever to the modern-day county. At that time, Britain was still attached to the European Continent, forming a north-west peninsula, and two main rivers ran roughly west to east across the region. The Ice Age, however, changed the shape of Suffolk forever. The Anglian Glaciation, which formed the extreme southern edge of a thick ice sheet that covered most of England, blanketed the majority of Suffolk. Roughly 10,000 years ago, when the ice finally retreated, it left a deep deposit of boulder clay on the central part of Suffolk. The resulting water from the melting, several hundred-metre-thick ice drained east and south-east, leaving the valleys now occupied by four of our major rivers: the Deben, Gipping, Stour and Waveney. And so, the basic – albeit bare – landscape of the county was formed.

About two-thirds of the county is covered by chalky boulder clay and the rest, to the east, by sands, silty clays and flint-rich gravels. When the ice finally disappeared, successive periods of warming of the climate allowed vegetation to grow on the bare rocks and a forest of birch and pine covered the land. This gradually gave way to mixed oak forests as the soil developed. Three distinct soil regions of Suffolk emerged; Breckland in the north-west, which comprised mainly heathland; the Sandlings in the south-east; and the claylands of High Suffolk, which became the main agricultural belt. And our county's most distinctive feature, its coastline, took shape when the land bridge between Britain and the Continent was finally broken in about 6500 BC.

PAKEFIELD MAN

So, when did man first set foot in Suffolk? Well, of course, we don't actually know, although humans were certainly here before the Ice Age, having migrated through Europe from East Africa. In 2000, the base of cliffs at Pakefield near Lowestoft yielded up some human-worked flints that have been dated to about 700,000 years ago. At the time of their discovery, they were the earliest evidence of humans in northern Europe. Since then, however, slightly older evidence has been found on the north Norfolk coast. Nevertheless, Suffolk can still lay claim to some of the country's earliest settlers and Pakefield certainly is not the only place in the county in which early, basic flint tools have been found. At numerous sites in the north-west corner of Suffolk, hand-axes have been unearthed that give us an insight into our early, pre-Ice Age ancestors. These people would have hunted horses and deer for their meat, as well as animals long since gone from our shores such as lions, bears and mammoths. As well as cutting up their prey, their crude flint tools were used to scrape the animal hide from which they made their clothing. It was not until the very end of the Ice Age that Suffolk was once again visited by early man, as well as by the animals upon which they relied for food.

THE FIRST SUFFOLK FARMERS

In around 4500 BC, crop cultivation and animal rearing began in Britain. In Suffolk, signs of these Neolithic farmers have been found predominantly in the Brecklands and Sandlings, as well as in river valleys in the rest of the county. These new skills had spread from the Near East, from where seeds and livestock had been imported. They grew wheat, barley, beans and flax, and kept cattle, sheep, goats and pigs. Woodland was cleared to allow for fields and pastures. With these new practices came the need for farmers to store their produce and so pottery-making emerged. Finds in Suffolk dating from this period show that the farmers also had to create new tools, some from stone other than flint, including those used for grinding corn.

Archaeological digs have also revealed evidence of Suffolk's earliest buildings. Although these finds are merely of pits, ditches, earthworks and post-holes, it demonstrates that these farming communities were established enough to put down roots in one place and to try to make themselves as comfortable as possible.

Crop marks, which emerge in our fields today at certain times of the year, include signs of a circular enclosure at Freston near Ipswich that may have been used by these people as a communal meeting place.

BARROWS AND BRONZE

It is thought that at least 825 barrows existed in Suffolk, although only just over 100 of these are visible today. Most of these earthen burial mounds were to be found in the previously populated areas of the county. Round barrows are the earliest surviving man-made features in our landscape and mainly date from the early Bronze Age (although some were built during the earlier Neolithic era). These burial places of our ancestors would contain from one to fifteen bodies or cremated remains. From bones found in these barrows, we know much about

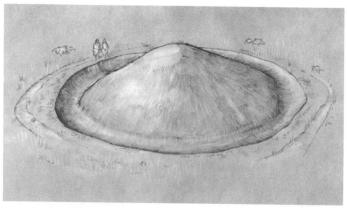

A round Bronze Age barrow.

our Suffolk forebears. The average age of death for men was 34, whereas for women it was 37½. Their average height was smaller than modern-day man at 5ft 7½in and women at 5ft 4in.

Sadly, there is little surviving evidence of Bronze Age settlements, but a group of sites has been excavated in West Row Fen near Mildenhall. These have revealed post-holes that tell us that some of the earliest known Suffolk houses were circular, about 5m in diameter, with square porches to protect the entrances.

It is also in the Bronze Age that we see the first creep of the population into the large swathe of Suffolk then still covered in forests growing on the heavy clay. These trees provided much-needed wood for the furnaces in which the new metal implements and tools were made. Although most of the metalwork finds still come from the north-west and south-east, drinking and cooking vessels, equipment needed for hunting, and horse harnesses have been found across the county.

WHEN TWO TRIBES GO TO WAR

Iron Age Suffolk was occupied by two major British tribes of people: the Iceni in the north and the (lesser-known) Trinovantes in the south. The Trinovantes were a Celtic tribe who were based in Colchester, although we know from the distribution of coins found that their territory extended into Suffolk as far north as roughly a line from Newmarket in the west to Aldeburgh on the coast. Iceni coinage that has been uncovered demonstrates that this tribe controlled the whole of Norfolk, as well as the northern part of Suffolk. Despite the fiercely defended territories of these tribes, experts believe there was a degree of encroachment into each other's lands, particularly by the Iceni into the south-east of the county.

Although we know very little about conflict between the Iceni and the Trinovantes, evidence of a couple of Iron Age hill fort sites have been discovered – at Burgh near Woodbridge and in Barnham. These suggest that there was a need to defend their land from neighbours intent on incursion. And the discovery, in 2008, of a hoard of gold coins in a large pottery jar near Wickham Market suggests a hurried burial of a treasury during an invasion. This stash of 840 gold coins produced by the Iceni tribe between 20 BC and AD 15 is the largest find of Iron Age coins in Britain since the 1800s. The Iceni were then led by Queen Boudica, whose reputation as a formidable ruler is backed up by a surviving description of her by the Roman historian Tacitus. He wrote that she was 'very tall and severe ... [with] long red hair that fell to her hips'. Although Boudica and her tribe of Iceni warriors had, at first, held out fiercely against the Romans (unlike the Trinovantes), they were eventually conquered by the invading army.

VENI, VIDI, VICI

The question often asked of the Romans is 'so, what did they ever do for us?'. Well, for a start they created around 400 miles of roads in the county, which formed a network of straight routes from the Romans' main East Anglian urban centres such as Colchester and Caistor St Edmund, as well as to other large settlements. In Suffolk these were probably in Long Melford,

Coddenham, Hacheston, Pakenham and Icklingham, as well as in Scole, a village on the border with Norfolk. The Romans built forts in some of these strategic locations. At Pakenham in mid-Suffolk, a large triple-ditched fort was unearthed. Archaeological digs in these places have uncovered high-status villas. These would have been the centre of a large estate comprising many smaller homesteads. Many of the excavations have also revealed significant industrial activity during the four centuries of Roman rule, including brewing, metalworking and pottery-making.

The extent of Roman settlement in Suffolk, however, reached further than just a handful of larger communities. More than 1,000 Roman sites – many of which would have been farmsteads – have been recorded across the county; probably just the tip of the iceberg. And they used the natural resources available in different parts of the region to their advantage. For instance, around the villages of Wattisfield and Rickinghall, which lie on rich clay, evidence of Roman pottery kilns has been found in abundance.

Roman rule in eastern England was not without its tribulations, such as civil war and internal revolts, as well as threats of invasion. These included attempted raids on the British coast by Germanic pirates. As a result, the Romans built a system of defences along the coastline, comprising a string of heavily defended fortresses. Two of these were in Suffolk, at Walton near Felixstowe and at Burgh Castle in the north-eastern tip of the county (now in Norfolk).

Like earlier Suffolk residents, the Romans buried large collections of coins and other treasured possessions, presumably when fears of being overthrown loomed. Several large hoards have been uncovered over the years including at Hoxne, where the remains of a wooden chest were found. It contained a large collection of gold, silver and bronze coins, as well as other gold and silver objects. But the most impressive of Suffolk's caches is the so-called Mildenhall Treasure, which is one of the most important finds ever of silver tableware from the late-Roman empire. The thirty-four objects of almost pure silver were dug up by a local farmer and his ploughman in 1942, although it took four years for the importance of the hoard to be recognised. It was subsequently declared 'treasure trove' and acquired by the British Museum.

THE SOUTH FOLK

It was after the end of Roman occupation of Britain that the new Anglo–Saxon kingdom of East Anglia was created. In his famous history of Britain completed in AD 731, the Northumbrian monk and scholar Bede refers to the *Provincial Orientalium Anglorum*. Bede also tells us that the Angles were Germanic migrants who brought with them a language that we know today as English. Sometime later, East Anglia was divided into two. And so, Suffolk, land of the South Folk (as opposed to Norfolk occupied by the North Folk) came into existence. The Waveney and Little Ouse rivers formed a natural boundary between the two areas, just as they do today. We don't know what exactly distinguished the South Folk from their northern neighbours, but it is possible that the two areas were simply made up of a different mix of migrants to East Anglia from various northern European countries.

The ruling family of East Anglia from around AD 550 was the Wuffingas, who claimed to be descended from both Julius Caesar and Woden, one of the main pagan gods. Their principal seat of power was at Rendlesham near Woodbridge. Recent excavations have revealed a wealth of high-quality objects dating from this time, including those made of gold with settings of precious stones. The number and quality of the Anglo–Saxon coins found at this large site is also remarkable, making it one of the wealthiest uncovered in England. Other remains found during the digs, including bones of young cattle (veal) and sparrowhawk skeletons, suggesting the aristocratic sport of falconry, also point to a high-profile, royal settlement.

The most distinguished king of the Wuffingas was Raedwald and it is now thought that he was buried at nearby Sutton Hoo, which is often called England's 'Valley of the Kings'. The discoveries at Sutton Hoo were made just before the Second World War by the self-taught archaeologist, Basil Brown. He had been engaged by the then owner of the land, Edith Pretty, to investigate some of the mounds on the estate, which she felt sure contained something of interest. After finding three previously robbed burials or cremation burials dating from the sixth or early seventh centuries, Basil Brown came across the remains of an undisturbed wooden ship burial that had been held together with iron rivets. He eventually excavated a whole 27 metre-long ship, which revealed a burial chamber. A host of treasures, including the now-iconic iron warrior's helmet, were found surrounding the skeleton. These Sutton Hoo treasures are now in a purpose-built gallery in the British Museum.

The early seventh-century Sutton Hoo helmet.

But what of ordinary Anglo–Saxon folk? Well, we are lucky that one of the earliest settlements of the English people has been unearthed in West Stow near Bury St Edmunds. Since its discovery in the 1960s, the site has been recreated to provide visitors with an insight into how our early forebears lived. The village had a mix of different types of timber buildings; the largest were for communal living and sleeping, and smaller ones were used for activities such as cooking and occupations such as weaving. Such reconstructions bridge the gap of time, bringing the past to the present.

CHRISTIANITY COMES TO SUFFOLK

Up until the late Roman period, Suffolk's people were pagan. Christianity, however, was made official by the Emperor Constantine in AD 313 and it seems that this new religion quickly seeped into every corner of the empire. Interestingly, in both the Mildenhall Treasure and the Hoxne Hoard, which in the main are decorated with pagan gods, goddesses and the like, some pieces have Christian inscriptions on them. Similarly, Icklingham near Mildenhall appears to have been both a pagan religious centre and then the site of a fourth-century Christian church. In 1974, a cemetery was uncovered with the skeletons oriented east–west in the Christian tradition. Outlines of buildings were also found, one of which appears to have housed a font used for Christian baptism and the other may have been an early church.

One of the earliest and most revered of East Anglian saints was St Botolph who was a Saxon who had been sent to a Benedictine Abbey in France to be educated.

On his return, the Saxon king granted him some land on which to found a monastery. Although the location of this monastery is disputed, most historians accept that it was at Iken near Aldeburgh. After St Botolph's death in AD 680, the abbey lived on for a further two centuries before it was destroyed by Viking invaders.

GIPESWIC

The county town of Suffolk claims to be the oldest continuously occupied English town. Ipswich was founded in the late sixth or early seventh century on the north bank of the River Orwell, one of a number of small Anglo–Saxon settlements near where the River Gipping flows into the Orwell estuary. It emerged as a 'wic' or 'emporium'; essentially a port that traded goods with similar centres across the North Sea. And so Gipeswic was formed. Its early economy was based on manufacturing and in the eighth century the most important industry was pottery-making. So-called 'Ipswich-ware' supplied the whole of East Anglia as well as further afield.

Archaeological digs have established that Anglo–Saxon Ipswich covered about 50 hectares (compared with today's sprawl of more than 4,000 hectares). The early layout of the streets is also reflected in the modern-day road system. St Stephen's Lane, for example, follows the course of an Anglo–Saxon path, alongside which post-holes from timber-framed houses have been found. As pagan practices gave way to wide-spread Christianity, it is likely that the town had one or more places of worship, possibly on the site of some of its current churches.

ST EDMUND, PATRON SAINT OF ENGLAND

Although many people have heard of St Edmund, it is a lesser-known fact that he was the first patron saint of England, before he lost his title to St George. Before his martyrdom, he was King Edmund of East Anglia and reigned for fourteen years until his death in AD 869. Edmund had reluctantly led his army into battle with a Danish invasion force. Local legend has it that, after being defeated in battle, Edmund hid under the Goldbrook Bridge in Hoxne. The reflection of his golden spurs glinting in the water revealed his hiding place to a newly-wed couple crossing the bridge. The couple informed the Danes, who promptly captured Edmund and demanded he renounce his Christian faith in favour of paganism. When he refused to do so, he was tied to a nearby oak tree. After whipping him, the Danes shot arrows at him until he was entirely covered. Even then he would not forsake Christ and so was beheaded, and the head was thrown into the woods. King Edmund's followers had no problem finding his body, but his head was missing. Searching for his remains, they heard a cry of 'here, here, here' and traced the voice to a wolf who was protecting Edmund's severed head. The wolf allowed them to take the head and they buried him nearby, building a wooden chapel over the spot. Many years later, after the threat from the Danes had ceased, they recovered Edmund and found his body

A medieval illumination depicting the martyrdom of King Edmund.

was as sound as if he were alive, including a completely healed neck.

The king's body was moved several times before finally coming to rest in a monastery at Bedricesworth which had been founded by King Sigeberht, son of the great King Raedwald. Within living memory of Edmund's death, he was accepted as a saint and special memorial coins were struck. The monastery became a place of great pilgrimage. The cult of St Edmund grew quickly and sometime around the beginning of the eleventh century, Bedricesworth was renamed Bury St Edmunds.

In Hoxne a great oak tree stood for around 1,000 years until it fell in 1848. The tree's trunk was more than 20ft in circumference. When the tree was cut up, it is said that an old arrowhead was found deep within the tree, 5ft from the base. Today, a stone cross marks the spot where the tree stood with an inscription 'St Edmund the Martyr AD 870. Oak tree fell August 1848 by its own weight'. There are, however, several other competing claims to the place of Edmund's death, including Bradfield St Clare.

SCANDINAVIAN SUFFOLK

It is a little-known fact that, for a period of around twenty-six years, Suffolk, and England, was under Danish rule, ended only by the accession of Edward the Confessor. Suffolk had borne the brunt of the various invasion attempts by the Danes; Ipswich had twice been in the direct firing line and had suffered greatly at the hands of the invaders.

Christianity made a speedy recovery when the Danes finally left and, by the time of the Norman invasion of Britain in 1066, East Anglia was divided into numerous administrative entities that had been formalised by the church. An existing Anglo–Saxon framework of villages and towns was used to create more than 500 ecclesiastical parishes, the smallest unit in the church hierarchy. The population had grown steadily, and the land was intensively farmed. In many cases, the Anglo–Saxon parish boundaries have remained largely unchanged over the centuries. And so, by the eleventh century the basic land- and townscape was approaching something we would recognise as Suffolk today. Even the names of many of the county's villages and towns were already established.

WHAT'S IN A NAME?

Unlike some other counties in England, the effect of the Norman Conquest on place names in Suffolk was minimal. Most of the names of our towns and villages have their origin in Anglo–Saxon Old English. At this time, names were given to single-family farmsteads that later grew into parishes and village names. In Suffolk we have a concentration of names ending in 'ham', which simply means 'a village or group of houses'. The ending 'ton' also had the same meaning, as in Kenton, Kedington and Moulton. We also have names incorporating 'ing'. This denotes groups of people, often the followers of a certain named individual. We therefore get interesting names such as Helmingham, which would have meant 'the farmstead of the family or people of a man called Helm'.

Anglo–Saxon personal names were used frequently in Suffolk such as in Edwardstone, Saxmundham and Woolverstone. The element 'ing' could also mean inhabitants of a particular locality. We therefore get place names such as Wratting, which means 'dwellers where the wort grows'. In fact, Suffolk has quite a number of other place names derived from plants and animals that describe the natural environment in which the place was set, such as Woolpit (wolf), Yaxley (cuckoo), Bentley (bent-grass) and Bramfield (broom).

2

NORMAN SUFFOLK

The defeat of King Harold by William the Conqueror on the Sussex coast in 1066 is often seen as a new chapter in English history. However, whilst power at the Royal court shifted from one dynasty to another, much of the country William governed continued relatively unchanged. Early eleventh-century England was not particularly stable, having had weak rulers such as Ethelred the Unready and Edward the Confessor. The arrival, therefore, of William led to far more organised times, albeit at the expense of the ruthlessness with which he ruled. His early years as king, however, were by no means peaceful. A Danish invasion force reached East Anglia in 1069 but was ultimately defeated near Ipswich, and the first Norman earl of East Anglia unsuccessfully plotted rebellion against William in 1076.

By the time of the Norman invasion, Suffolk already had most of the settlements that became our present-day villages. The county also had basic infrastructure and an administrative system that has also stood the test of time. The Normans, therefore, merely stamped their mark on Suffolk rather than fundamentally shaping it.

LITTLE DOMESDAY

The Domesday Book, which King William I ordered to be compiled in 1086 and which is England's oldest surviving public record, is a snapshot of people and places as they had been in the late Anglo–Saxon period. It records the name of the king's main landholders (tenants-in-chief), their manors and estates, as well as the amount of tax and rents payable to the monarch. It is a comprehensive survey and valuation of landholding and resources in late eleventh-century England.

The Domesday volumes that survive today include the so-called 'Little Domesday', which covers Suffolk as well as Norfolk and Essex. It was probably a working copy that was intended to be summarised for inclusion in the main Domesday survey. However, it was never included in the 'Great Domesday' and so the draft was kept. 'Little Domesday' contains far greater detail than for the other parts of the country covered in the main volume, which allows us an invaluable insight into life in Suffolk at the beginning of the second millennium.

In Domesday Suffolk, we find listed around 640 separate settlements. The main urban centres were Ipswich, Bury St Edmunds, Dunwich, Eye, Beccles, Clare and Sudbury. Not all individuals are counted in the survey; only landowners, their tenants and the people they controlled. From the 20,000 or so who are counted, it could be assumed the population of Suffolk was very roughly 100,000. And it wasn't only people who were counted; we can glean a lot of fascinating information about the livestock farmed for food and other commodities. In addition to numerous oxen used to pull the ploughs, 37,522 sheep are listed, as well as 4,343 goats, whilst only nine cows and two donkeys are enumerated (although there were probably more).

WHO'S WHO OF THE ELEVENTH CENTURY

Since the purpose of Domesday was to establish which of the king's subjects held land and how much they owed him for their estate holdings, all the upper echelons of society are named in the survey. There were seventy-one tenants-in-chief listed in Suffolk, of whom twenty-one held lands in Norfolk and Essex as well. These tenants-in-chief were the king's barons, bishops and abbots who rented land from William. In turn, many sub-let to named individuals. Nobody below this level is mentioned by name in the document.

It is not surprising that most of the people named in Domesday Suffolk were Norman–French. A few English names appear but only in very minor positions. As well as King William himself, who directly controlled great swathes of the county including Ipswich, we find the king's half-brother, Robert of Mortain, Count Alan of Brittany and William de Warenne. There were three other major tenants-in-chief who had important and sizeable holdings. Richard de Clare, Chief Justice to the monarch, received ninety-five lordships in Suffolk alone (and seventy-five elsewhere). The castle and borough of Clare became the centre of his operations. Roger Bigod received 117 Suffolk manors; his descendants, who became the Earls of Norfolk in the twelfth century, administered the estate from four castles: at Bungay, Framlingham, Ipswich and Walton. William Malet, who had 221 holdings in the county, had as his main residence the castle and borough of Eye.

GREEN ENERGY

We tend to think that harnessing nature to provide energy is a modern-day invention, aimed at preserving dwindling resources such as coal and oil. However, mills were commonplace in eleventh-century Suffolk. About one-third of all the county's settlements mentioned in Domesday Book had a mill. Although some might have been animal-powered millstones, most were watermills; windmills were not introduced into Britain until after the survey. We have archaeological evidence of watermills dating back to the seventh century and we know that the Romans too used water power.

Pakenham watermill is one of the oldest surviving mills still working in England. Although the current building only dates from the eighteenth century, we know from Domesday that there was a watermill in the village at the time of the Norman invasion, very probably at the same point on the river as it now stands. Such mills were controlled by the landowner and all their residents would have to pay to take their grain to be milled.

Suffolk is also home to one of the first tide mills in the country, and definitely the last one still in operation. This is at Woodbridge on the River Deben. The earliest record of a mill on the site is in 1170, although it may have been there for some time before this date. A tide mill is driven by tidal rise and fall. A dam with a sluice is created across a suitable tidal inlet, or a

Woodbridge Tide Mill.

section of river estuary is made into a reservoir. As the
tide comes in, it enters the mill pond through a one-
way gate, and this gate closes automatically when the
tide begins to fall. Both Pakenham and Woodbridge
mills were owned by one of the main landowners in
Suffolk at that time, the Church; Pakenham by the
Abbey of Bury St Edmunds and Woodbridge by the local
Augustinian priory.

THE POWER OF RELIGION

Although the established Christian church in England
was little over a few centuries old, by 1086 a large

proportion of Suffolk was owned by religious houses. The Benedictine Abbey of Ely held several manors scattered all over the county and had a stronghold in south-east Suffolk. The Archbishop of Canterbury, along with two French bishops and the English bishops of Thetford and Rochester, also held Suffolk land. But by far the most powerful and influential landowner was the Abbey of Bury St Edmunds, which held about 300 separate manors and estates in Suffolk, Norfolk, Essex and elsewhere in the country.

The Benedictine Abbey of Bury St Edmunds had been established in 1020 and Edward the Confessor had substantially enhanced the abbey's privileges. So, by the time of the Norman Conquest, the abbey ranked fourth among English abbeys in wealth and political importance. The Normans replaced the Saxon church on a grand scale and then the spectacular west front was completed around the turn of the thirteenth century under Abbot Samson, who also added a great central tower and lower octagonal towers to either side. He also improved the accommodation, including a new hall to house the abbey's many monastic visitors. We know much of Abbot Samson's leadership of the abbey because of a fascinating, surviving chronicle written by one of the monks, Jocelyn de Brakelond. In his account, he records the politics and practicalities of monastic life between 1173 and 1202. The 'hero' of the account is undoubtedly Abbot Samson who, in administering the abbey's far-reaching estate, according to Jocelyn:

> ... restored the old halls and ruined houses, through which kites and crows flew; he built new chapels, and rooms and seats in

many places where there had never been buildings, save perhaps barns. He also made many parks, which he filled with beasts, and had a huntsman and dogs. He made many clearings and brought land into cultivation, in everything regarding the advantage of the abbacy ... For the management of the same manors and for the management of all other affairs, he appointed monks and laymen who were wiser than those who had previously held the posts, and who made careful provision for us and our lands.

SUFFOLK AT PRAYER

During the Norman rule in England, there was a growth in religious orders and their houses. In Suffolk, despite the domination of the great abbey at Bury St Edmunds,

Butley Priory as it was in 1785.

many smaller religious institutions were founded, including nine further Benedictine monasteries and nunneries, such as at Eye. Thirteen Augustinian priories sprung up, the largest being at Ixworth and Butley, and other orders founded communities such as the Cistercians at Sibton and the Premonstratensians in Leiston.

The Normans also rebuilt many parish churches that had been founded in the Anglo–Saxon era. As the French eleventh-century chronicler Ralph Glaber wrote, 'it was as though the very world had shaken herself and cast off her old age, and was now clothing herself in a white robe of new churches'. By the time of the Domesday survey, Suffolk had about 418 churches, by far the greatest number of any county in England (for instance, Norfolk had only 274). Churches that have been in continual use since then have, of course, been updated, repaired and extended many times in the intervening centuries and so much of the surviving Norman building details are hidden or disguised behind later walls, doorways and windows. That said, many examples of original Norman church doorways survive, such as at Wissett and the now-ruined chancel at Orford. They are recognisable by their round arches and zig-zag decoration.

One striking feature of some Suffolk churches that date from the Norman period is the round tower; the county has forty-two round-tower churches, although some were built in the later medieval period. With the construction of stone churches – as opposed to earlier wooden structures – came the building of towers to house bells. The bells, with different modes of ringing for different occasions, were used to call parishioners to prayer and to mark the hours for celebrations, as well as for funerals. While we don't know for sure why round towers were preferred, particularly in East Anglia, it is believed that it was simply because they were relatively easy to build with the materials that were available locally. With flint being the most readily available building material in Suffolk, it can be set into mortar to provide an attractive finish, whereas it cannot so easily be worked or cut to provide the edges required for a square tower.

A NORMAN'S HOME IS HIS CASTLE

One of the most enduring of Norman legacies in Suffolk are the castles. Although there were such fortifications around before the invasion, the numerous Norman lords who had been granted land by William the Conqueror quickly set about constructing a castle to defend their territory. Of course, the imposing structures they built also served as an important status symbol. A typical Norman (motte-and-bailey) castle comprised a stone, fortified structure – the keep – that was built on raised earthwork. Attached to this would have been an enclosed courtyard where ancillary buildings would have stood. All that remains of many such castles are either some ruins of the keep or even just the earthen mound.

Although Domesday Book mentions just one castle in Suffolk – at Eye – probably more than this existed, including at Haughley and Clare. Earthwork evidence of many smaller castles has been found across the county, all of which have long since disappeared. One castle that survives in part is at Bungay. It was built in 1140 during

Framlingham Castle.

the reign of King Stephen, when a spate of new castles appeared during a period of civil war. It has the thickest walls of any surviving castle in England. On the Suffolk coast at Orford is one of the best examples of a twelfth-century stone keep. It was constructed by King Henry II and cost £1,407 to build. Orford was a new development in castle design in that the structure has less defined corners than earlier square keeps. But undoubtedly the finest existing castle in the county is at Framlingham. This stronghold was built by Hugh Bigod (who also owned the castle at Bungay) sometime before 1148 in the Norman motte-and-bailey style and was probably constructed on the site of an earlier fortification. However, this structure was ordered to be destroyed by Henry II, following Bigod's involvement in a rebellion. Eventually, though, a replacement was built by Roger Bigod, Duke of Norfolk, in the latter years of the twelfth century using the new fashion of a tall curtain-wall with thirteen flanking towers. Despite this building being better designed to repel attack, Framlingham's castle was successfully captured by King John in 1216 after a short siege.

3

MEDIEVAL SUFFOLK

During the medieval period, Suffolk underwent a huge transformation in almost every walk of life. Compared to other parts of the country it was relatively populous and remained so for many centuries. However, like other counties, it first had to endure several crises before it emerged revived and re-energised economically, socially and religiously. During the reigns of Edward I and Edward II, social unrest bubbled up, mainly in Bury St Edmunds. These uprisings were finally subdued but these were early signs of the people flexing their muscles against the might of the establishment. It was the effect of the devastating plague that swept through the southern and eastern counties of England in the fourteenth century, however, which proved a major trigger for further riots later that century.

It was also during this period, though, that Suffolk emerged as an industrial powerhouse, creating a wealthy merchant class with an eye on their social and religious well-being. These people were largely responsible for the architectural gems in the form of houses and large churches. Moreover, the county was endowed with a seemingly endless supply of skilled craftsmen who took pride in their creations. Suffolk's coastline, too, was an economic goldmine, although the battle with the force of nature was, at times, lost.

CLOTH EQUALS WEALTH

It is widely thought that Suffolk's medieval dominance in the cloth trade was due to the arrival of Flemish weavers in the 1330s. However, whilst these immigrants undoubtedly influenced the industry in Norwich and Chelmsford, they do not seem to have contributed to the already flourishing cloth-making in Suffolk. As early as the beginning of the 1200s, Jocelyn de Brakelond of the Abbey of Bury St Edmunds recorded in his chronicle the use of the two rivers in the town for the fulling process (where the cloth is cleansed of impurities, making it thicker). Fulling mills in Hadleigh (which lies on the River Brett) and Sudbury (on the River Stour), as well as in Bury (with the rivers Lark and Linnet), were well established by the beginning of the fourteenth century. The woollen cloth industry was a major employer in the south-west corner of the county, from Clare in the west to East Bergholt in the east, taking in Lavenham, Nayland, Glemsford and Long Melford. The cloth manufacturers – the clothiers – offered employment to large numbers of men, women and children in the range of processes required to produce the finished product, such as shearing, carding, dyeing, spinning and weaving. Much of this work was undertaken in the worker's own home.

A visitor today to the former cloth-making towns in Suffolk does not have to look very far to find evidence of the great wealth that was generated from this industry in the late Middle Ages. Whole streets are lined with fine timber-framed houses and many boast impressive wool halls and guildhalls, built to provide indoor market facilities, as well as an administrative centre for the medieval equivalents of trades unions.

SUFFOLK'S COASTAL POWER

The late medieval period saw the undoubted heyday of Suffolk's coastal power in terms of international trade. Iceland, relatively easily accessible from the Suffolk coast, provided a market in dried fish. Gascony, on the Bay of Biscay, offered a profitable trading route in wines. The numerous ports along the Suffolk coastline also played a key role in the defence of the country. In 1294, for example, Edward I ordered that twenty-six towns on the east and south coasts, including Ipswich and Dunwich, should provide boats for a fleet to fight the French. The port of Ipswich was frequently called upon to supply merchant ships for the king's fleet.

At the time of Domesday Book in 1086, Dunwich was a thriving town – the tenth largest place in England, with a population one-sixth the size of London. It was a naval base and a religious centre with many large churches, monasteries, hospitals and grand public buildings. Dunwich residents grew wealthy from trade, shipbuilding and a large, seventy-vessel fishing fleet. However, even then there was evidence of significant coastal erosion, although at the same time as the cliffs were being worn away, a spit of land was created that provided a perfect harbour. In the next few centuries, Dunwich

The remains of Greyfriars, a Franciscan friary in Dunwich.

became a highly successful fishing and mercantile trading port. By 1250 it was one of the largest ports in England with a population of 4,000 people in thirteen parishes. Dunwich's decline, however, began in 1286 when a storm hit the Suffolk coast. This was followed by two further storms a year later. Because of this extreme weather, the Dunwich river's exit into the sea shifted a few miles north to Walberswick. Coupled with the destruction of the safe harbour and buildings in Dunwich, the maritime business in the town started to take a rapid downturn. Most of the medieval buildings have now disappeared into the sea, including all eight churches, and today Dunwich has fewer than fifty permanent residents, reducing a once great port to a tiny fishing village.

THE COMMERCIAL REVOLUTION

The rapid growth of industry in Suffolk led to the equally brisk foundation of local markets. Domesday Book lists just nine market towns, but between 1227 and 1310 it is believed royal charters were granted for around seventy markets in the county. Such charters were legal documents formally giving permission for the village or town to hold a market on a given day (or days). The charter also often allowed fairs to be held on saints' days of significance to the community. For instance, in Botesdale, King Henry III granted the lord of the manor, the Abbot of the Abbey of Bury St Edmunds, the right to hold a market every Thursday. He was also permitted to hold a fair once a year on the eve and day of the feast of St Botolph, 17 June. In Botesdale, like other Suffolk market towns, it is thought that the royal charter merely formalised an existing arrangement that stretched back many decades or centuries. However, some markets, such as the one held in Haverhill, never received legal recognition, while some communities that were granted charters never held a market, such as Felsham and Wissett.

The sites chosen for a market varied greatly but, in an age where there was increased mobility on the road networks, an obvious choice was alongside a major road or at a bridging point on a river. Understandably, there was much competition between neighbouring markets, and a thirteenth-century lawyer had even recommended that a distance of at least 6.6 miles be maintained between markets. Despite this, there was a cluster of six markets in the east of Suffolk in an area just 6 miles across. In central Suffolk, Hoxne struggled to compete with the market in nearby Eye. In Norman times, both had held markets and both originally on a Saturday. Hoxne had therefore been forced to move its market to a Friday and in 1227, a charter moved the market day again, to a Wednesday. This may have been due to the fact that almost at the same time, neighbouring Stradbroke and Laxfield were also given permission to hold markets on Friday and Saturday respectively.

Inevitably, given such fierce competition over time, some markets managed to continue until the present day while others ceased. By the seventeenth century, around a half of medieval markets were still held and a number of others ceased to function in the following two centuries.

BREEDING LIKE RABBITS

The ultimate in medieval money-making ventures was farming rabbits for their meat and fur. This was particularly so for those who needed to derive an income from the sandy soils of the Brecklands and Sandlings in northwest Suffolk, which were ill-suited to arable farming. Rabbit meat was then a prized delicacy, eaten at the royal court as well as by wealthy noblemen across the country, and its fur was used as trimming for clothes as well as for warm hats. Black and silver-grey rabbit pelt was particularly sought after. Rabbits are not native to Britain but were first introduced by the Romans, although they seem to have died out and were reintroduced by the Normans. Since rabbits, or 'coneys', as mature rabbits were known, were easy prey to predators, they had to be kept in walled or fenced areas called warrens. To be a warrener, then, was an important job. These well-paid employees

Mildenhall warren lodge.

had to feed the rabbits and bore holes to encourage the animals to burrow, as well as warding off both predators and poachers.

Many of the medieval warrens were established by monasteries or large landholders and these rabbit farms swelled their coffers considerably. Some of the largest were in the Breckland area of Suffolk. To the east of Mildenhall, a substantial warren was held by the Abbey of Bury St Edmunds. A recently restored medieval warren lodge stands on a high point where the warren was located. It is a square, two-storey stone building and is typical of the structures built to house the warrener. As well as providing accommodation, there was secure storage space for the carcasses and pelts as well as the equipment needed to trap the rabbits. It also served as a lookout and defence against poachers.

After the Dissolution of the Monasteries in the six-teenth century, most warrens passed into the hands of landowners, who continued rabbit farming, in a few cases in Suffolk, well into the twentieth century.

THE BEGINNINGS OF HUMAN RIGHTS

The county of Suffolk played a key role in one of the defining moments of England's history: the drawing up of, and royal assent to, the Magna Carta. Following King John's loss of some of his main continental land holdings in the early years of the thirteenth century, the monarch set about raising the money he needed to recover this territory. One way to bring in this much-needed revenue was to push his manorial rights over his earls and barons to the limit. These members of the aristocracy held their land directly from the king in return for pledging allegiance to him, as well as providing military service. Below them was a further hierarchical structure, down to the tenants and peasants who farmed the land. The king demanded of his earls and barons higher taxes on property transactions on their estates. Faced with crip-pling financial obligations to King John, twenty-five barons emerged as rebels demanding fairer treatment. Of these, five were Suffolk landholders: Roger and Hugh Bigod, the father and son holders of Framlingham Castle, William de Huntingfield, and Richard de Clare and his son, Gilbert.

The Borough of St Edmundsbury has as its motto *Sacrarium Regis, Cunabula Legis*, meaning 'Shrine of a King, Cradle of the Law'. Whilst the first part of the phrase refers to the martyred King Edmund, the second lays claim to Bury St Edmunds' crucial role in the drawing up of the Magna Carta. In November 1214, the rebel barons met in the Abbey at Bury St Edmunds. The chronicler Roger of Wendover in his *Floes Historiarum* (The Flowers of History) takes up the story:

> About this time the earls and barons of England assembled at St Edmund's as if for religious duties, although it was for some other reason; for after they had discoursed together secretly for a time, there was placed before them the charter of King Henry the First, which they had received, as mentioned before, in the City of London from Stephen, Archbishop of Canterbury. This charter contained certain liberties and laws granted to the holy church as well as the nobles of the kingdom, besides some liberties which the king added of his own accord. All therefore assembled in the church of St. Edmund the king and martyr, and commencing from those of the highest rank, they all swore on the great altar that, if the king refused to grant these liberties and laws, they themselves would withdraw from their allegiance to him, and make war on him, till he should, by a charter under his own seal, confirm to them everything they required; and finally it was unanimously agreed that, after Christmas, they should all go together to the king and demand the confirmation of the aforesaid liberties to them, and that they should in the meantime provide themselves with horses and arms so that if the king should endeavour to depart from his oath, they might by taking his castles compel him to satisfy their demands; and having arranged this, each man returned home.

The following year, and as a direct result of this meeting in Bury St Edmunds, King John sealed the Magna Carta. The resulting charter sought to impose limits on the king's powers over his subjects and enshrined in English political and legal practice the right of the individual.

A MANORIAL TENANT'S LOT

Compared with many other counties in England, Suffolk had a dense and growing population, due mainly to its rapidly rising fortunes. By the end of the thirteenth century, Suffolk inhabitants numbered around 140,000, double the population two centuries earlier. With this increased demand on the land for food, the manorial structure became the dominant force. The administrative heart of the manor was the lord's hall, in which he may or may not have lived, depending on how many manors he (or she) held. Here was where the manorial court sittings were held, which managed the day-to-day business of the estate, ranging from property disputes to accusations of trespass.

The lord's tenants were able to hold parcels of land and to farm them as they saw fit. In exchange, they were expected to undertake certain labour services for the lord, or to give money or goods in lieu of this work. These tenants were also able to sell their land or bequeath it on their death. All such transfers of land ownership were subject to a 'fine' to the lord of the manor. Many lords also had watermills and windmills where his tenants were obliged to pay to grind their corn. At Rattlesden, for example, a tenant with 20 acres of land was expected to pay twenty-nine and a half pennies in dues plus three hens at Christmas and twenty eggs at Easter. He also had to do two 'works', such as ploughing, mowing, cleaning ditches or making hurdles each week from October to August. There were further requirements including a personal tax, as well as an additional sum of money if his daughter married or if she had an illegitimate child. In fact, a manorial tenant's life was dominated by his or her obligations to their lord, and many eked out a very meagre existence.

PLAGUE!

In the spring of 1349, Suffolk was hit by the dreaded plague known as the Black Death. It had reached England from the Mediterranean in the summer of the previous year and by the following summer, Suffolk's population had decreased dramatically, by between a third and a half, in line with other counties in southern England. The infection stayed in the county throughout much of 1349, bringing tragedy to all levels of society and disruption to all walks of life. Manorial court records dating from this time provide us with a vivid picture of the extent to which whole families were wiped out by the Black Death. In the village of Walsham-le-Willows, 102 deaths of tenants were listed in June 1349, as opposed to no more than ten before the outbreak. In nearby Redgrave a month later, 169 deaths were reported. Higher up the social ladder, surviving records from the diocese of Norwich show that new priests appointed to churches in Suffolk reached a peak of 222 in July 1349, compared with an average of just three per month in the previous year.

The devastating effect of the Black Death was not only counted in human terms. The harvests of 1349, 1350 and 1351 were diminished not because of adverse weather conditions but because of the shortage of manpower to tend the land. Many landholdings were left vacant because no family member could be found immediately to inherit land of a plague victim. The epidemic was therefore followed by a period of fundamental economic change. Rental prices for land plummeted and wages rose steeply, fuelled by the scarcity of manual workers. Many labouring-class families took the opportunity to move to manors where lords were prepared to pay the highest wages and to offer smallholdings for minimal rent.

Suffolk was once again hit by plague in 1361, although deaths were considerably fewer than in 1349 and it appears to have struck mainly children. The county suffered frequent outbreaks of the plague in later centuries, but none had such a lasting effect as the Black Death.

RIOT!

In the second half of the fourteenth century, Suffolk people were still reeling from the shock of the Black Death. On top of this, the working classes were having to contend with strict controls on the level of wages, as well as high taxes. Nowadays, we think of the poll tax as a twentieth-century invention even though the first such tax was levied in 1377, the first year of the reign of Richard II. Unlike earlier taxes that targeted the relatively well-off, this tax on individuals covered the whole population of England, with only beggars and younger children being exempt. In 1380, the tax was three times higher than that of the previous year and, unlike its predecessor, taxed rich and poor at the same rate. Hence, it was particularly unpopular with the peasantry. With this backdrop, a major unrest broke out in the country that is widely known as the Peasants' Revolt of 1381. It was a movement in which Suffolk played a major part and was led not by the labouring class but, instead, by businessmen and professional men.

The Suffolk revolt was led by John Wrawe, chaplain of Sudbury. He and his mob stormed the Abbey of Bury St Edmunds, seizing the goods of the Lord Chief Justice, John de Cavendish, and beheading him. The acting Abbot of the abbey suffered the same fate. In London, an eminent Suffolk churchman, the then Archbishop of Canterbury, was seized and executed by rebels on Tower Hill. One of the most bizarre of relics of Simon of Sudbury (as he is known after his place of origin) is his pickled head, which is kept in St Gregory's church in his home town. The rebellion in its most intense phase lasted just eight days, being carefully timed to coincide with the feast day of Corpus Christi on 13 June. Around twenty people on both sides died in the Suffolk revolt, which was largely quashed by troops under the command of the Earl of Suffolk.

SUFFOLK DRAGONS

Ever since the written word has been used to record events, chroniclers have recorded both mundane occurrences such as battles, power struggles and Royal succession, as well as the more fantastical. Two early chronicles point to an interesting dragon hot-spot on the border of Suffolk and Essex near Sudbury. The first account involved Sir Richard Waldegrave, a Member of Parliament for Suffolk and Speaker of the House of Commons, in 1405. Sir Richard lived at Smallbridge Manor near Bures and encountered the monster first-hand. The chronicle reveals:

Close to the town of Bures there has lately appeared … a dragon vast in body with crested head, teeth like a saw and tail extending to an enormous length. Having slaughtered the shepherd, it devoured very many sheep. There came forth an order, to shoot at him with arrows, to the workmen on whose domain he had concealed himself being Sir Richard de Waldegrave, Knight, but the dragon's body although struck by the archers remained unhurt, for those arrows bounced off his back if it were been iron or hard rock. Those arrows that fell upon the spine gave out as they struck it a ringing or tinkling sound just as if they had hit a brazon plate and then flew away off by reason of the hide of the great beast being impenetrable. There was an order to destroy him and in all the country people assembled. But when the dragon saw he was again to be assaulted he fled away into a marsh or mere and was no more seen.

Some forty-four years later, according to an account in a manuscript now in the library of Canterbury Cathedral, a battle of the fire-breathing monsters occurred:

On Friday the 26th of September in the year of our Lord 1449, about the hour of Vespers, two terrible dragons were seen fighting for about the space of one hour, on two hills, of which one, in Suffolk, is called Kydyndon Hyl and the other in Essex Blacdon Hyl. One was black in colour and the other reddish and spotted. After a long conflict the reddish one obtained the victory over the black, which done, both returned into the hills above named whence they had come, that is to say, each to his own place to the admiration of many beholding them.

A PLACE IN HEAVEN

The medieval boom in trade and industry proved extremely beneficial to the church. Many parishioners whose industries were thriving believed that giving money to the fabric and upkeep of their church was good for their souls. All over Suffolk, either completely new parish churches were built, or else existing buildings were considerably extended and improved. The fifteenth century saw churches, in the new Perpendicular style of architecture, springing up along the coast, stretching from Lowestoft in the north to Aldeburgh in the south. The fishing community of Walberswick demonstrated their piety and wealth by funding a magnificent new church. They also contributed a share of the proceeds of their catch towards the upkeep of the building. Sadly, the decline of the fishing trade in the seventeenth century and the subsequent economic downturn of such coastal villages, saw the Walberswick population decrease dramatically. Their once-great church fell into disrepair. It was partially dismantled and stripped of its valuable assets such as the bells and stained-glass windows, which were transferred to a new, more modest church further inland.

Lavenham and Long Melford churches stand out as two of the finest examples of their kind financed by wealthy cloth merchants. In both cases, an existing church was remodelled and greatly expanded in the late 1400s. The main benefactors had themselves immortalised in the structure itself. At Lavenham the coat of arms of the Spring family, as well as the merchant's mark of Thomas Spring, the 13th Earl of Oxford, appears more than thirty times in the flintwork on the outside of

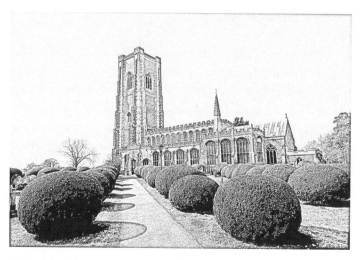

The parish church of St Peter and St Paul, Lavenham.

the church. Long Melford church has an entire portion devoted to its most prominent local family, the Cloptons. The cloth merchant John Clopton, who lived at nearby Kentwell Hall, financed the reconstruction of the church and therefore created a chapel in its north-east corner, using some of the older building, to commemorate various Clopton family members. A further, smaller chapel, called the Clopton Chantry Chapel, is attached to the main chapel. This holds the tomb of John Clopton and his wife.

All over Suffolk, wealthy merchants left considerable fortunes in their wills to establish chantry chapels. These were either attached to the existing parish church or sometimes constructed as free-standing buildings. Their purpose was to provide a place where priests were employed to sing masses for the soul of the founder of the chapel. Those who could not afford to found their own chapel would give provision in their will for a sum of money to pay for a priest to pray for them after their death. It was widely believed that after death, an individual's soul entered purgatory, a sort of intermediate state where those destined for heaven had to undergo purification. By leaving money for prayers, sermons and masses to be said for their soul, people believed that they would shorten the length of time they would spend in purgatory.

ANGELS ON HIGH

Of the almost 170 medieval angel roofs that survive in England and Wales, Suffolk boasts the largest number – around 29 per cent – closely followed by Norfolk. These angels are to be found in parish churches high above our heads and all were constructed in the fifteenth and early sixteenth centuries. Before Henry VIII broke with Rome in the 1530s, our churches were filled with carved and brightly coloured images ranging from rood screens with Christ and the saints, vivid wall paintings and stained glass depicting Biblical scenes. Whilst many of these were destroyed, defaced or whitewashed over either during the English Reformation or in the Puritan purge a century later, many of the stunning carved angel roofs survived, merely because they were out of reach.

The predominance of angel roofs in East Anglia is due, simply, to three factors. First, the will to undertake such ambitious projects was there, driven by gentry and merchants who wanted to demonstrate both their wealth and prestige, as well as their religious belief. Secondly, the region was the most prosperous in the country at this time and therefore had money to pay for these ambitious schemes. Lastly, East Anglian expertise in carpentry and wood carving was second to none. Many of Suffolk's angel roofs were made by local craftsmen who undertook both the carpentry for the roof itself, as well as the carving. However, master craftsmen would have been brought in from further afield to help with the larger building projects. Oak was favoured for the construction of the roofs, although other woods were occasionally used, for instance in Mildenhall where the roof is thought to be made of sycamore.

Some of the finest angel roofs in Suffolk are to be found in the churches at Bury St Edmunds, Cotton, Earl Stonham and Woolpit. The hammer beam roof at St Mary's Church in Bury St Edmunds is arguably the finest example in the country. The nave roof is adorned with twenty-two angels, who form a procession and carry all manner of objects used at High Mass such as incense burners, candles and bibles. There are choirmasters with hands raised as if conducting, young women bearing crowns, as well as two kings holding sceptres. At Woolpit there are no fewer than sixty-six angels on the double hammer beam nave roof with more than sixty more in the aisles. Sadly, the angels are mostly Victorian replacements of the originals, which may have disappeared sometime in the mid-sixteenth century.

MEDIEVAL GRAFFITI

In the Middle Ages it seems that scratching your name, an image or symbol onto the walls and columns in your local parish church was commonplace and almost encouraged, unlike today. Medieval churches were very different from the plain, whitewashed interiors we see today. Instead, they were a place of vibrancy and colour. Just about every surface would have had some sort of painted decoration on them. Even the lower sections of walls, which would be free from the highly decorative painted schemes, would be colour washed. Members of church congregations over the centuries carved personal graffiti onto these surfaces and these inscriptions would therefore have stood out very clearly against the bright pigments of the painted decoration. They would have been one of the most obvious things people entering the church would have noticed. This early church graffiti had both meaning and function. Far from being random doodling, they represent the prayers, memorials, hopes and fears of medieval communities.

The walls and pillars inside the church of St Mary, Lidgate are covered with surviving medieval graffiti. Among these, written in neat, small lettering on a column by the south door, is an intriguing Latin inscription. It translates as 'John Lydgate made this with licence on the day of St Simon and Jude'. Lydgate was a near contemporary of Geoffrey Chaucer, who was a monk at the nearby abbey at Bury St Edmunds. Other graffiti in Lidgate church, mirrored in other Suffolk churches, range from people, fish and other animals, windmills, ships, mason's and merchant's marks, and crosses and other religious symbols. But by far the cleverest piece of graffiti in Lidgate is one that combines musical notation, an image and text. It is a word puzzle or rebus and has taken some considerable effort to decipher. We now know that it creates the phrase WELL FARE MI LADY

CATERYNE (well fare my Lady Catherine). We do not know who scratched this clever piece of graffiti onto a column. Nor do we know when, or indeed the identity of Lady Catherine. We can only hazard a guess that it was either a simple message of good wishes or a public declaration of love or devotion.

PARISH, PRAYER AND PARTY

One institution that played a central role in the social and religious life of the medieval parish was the gild. These gilds were separate institutions from the craft and trades guilds that existed mainly in towns across the country and looked after the interests of crafts- and tradesmen. In Suffolk, we know that the majority of parishes had one or more religious gilds, making almost 500 in total. By being a member of a gild, a man or woman could claim financial help should they be unable to work and therefore struggle to feed themselves and their family. They also earned the right to be prayed for by gild members when they died.

Parish gilds were dedicated to a particular saint, and members would celebrate their saint's day as well as holding feasts and plays throughout the year. At first, these social activities of gilds were held inside churches, although this was frowned upon by some and, over time, special gildhalls were built. Sometimes a single hall would be used by more than one gild and because of the close relationship between gild and church, the first gildhalls tended to be built next to or near the church. Only a few records of Suffolk medieval gilds survive but those that do show they owned livestock, which was rented out to parishioners. The gild also employed cooks, as well as musicians to play for their celebrations.

A number of medieval gildhall buildings still stand today in Suffolk. When the gilds ceased operating – many in the 1540s when they were formally dissolved under an Act of Parliament – parishes bought the property and used it as a school or workhouse. Others passed into private ownership. The old gildhall in Eye is an impressive half-timbered house standing next to the parish church. It was used as the town's grammar school for nearly 500 years and is a private house today. The equally impressive old gildhall in Laxfield stands opposite the church and now houses a local museum.

In the Middle Ages, church ales were one of England's most traditional and festive forms of ecclesiastical fundraising. It seems perfectly natural to assume that those

Laxfield Gildhall.

people who worshipped together would also drink together. Where Suffolk does stand head and shoulders above many other counties, however, is in the wealth of surviving records and buildings that are testament to this custom. The surviving parish accounts of Cratfield tell us that church ales were hosted by Cratfield, or by neighbouring villages, between five and six times a year, raising substantial sums of money. This continued into the early sixteenth century. These festivities were traditionally held on Passion Sunday, Pentecost, All Saints' Day and Plough Monday. Another popular day for holding these celebrations was the Fourth Sunday in Lent, which is still sometimes called 'Refreshment Sunday'. On these occasions, ales were brewed, yeasty cakes were baked, and residents of villages nearby were invited to come and enjoy the day and, of course, buy the food and drink at inflated prices. The visitors didn't mind paying over the odds for their ale and cakes because they knew they could reciprocate on another occasion. Whilst the majority of the profit from Cratfield's ales appears to have been spent on the church building and ornaments, their church ales were sometimes sold to benefit an individual or a specific cause. Bride ales were sold on behalf of a newly married couple to give them a good financial start in life and help ales were brewed to assist a parishioner who had fallen on hard times.

4

TUDOR SUFFOLK

Whilst the Tudor period heralded a more stable Britain in the political sense, when it came to religion the sixteenth century witnessed constant upheaval and reform. Like the rest of the country, Suffolk suffered enormously at the English Reformation. The county's ornately decorated churches were defaced and the grip of power the monasteries had over Suffolk finally yielded. This heralded in an era where the landed gentry and those with new-found wealth consolidated and added to their estates. However, this led to discontent amongst the working classes at various times in the century as a result of their resentment of levels of taxation and land management.

Tudor Suffolk played host to a succession of royal visitors and residents. This demonstrates the importance of the county at this time. It was both a battleground and playground for Tudor monarchs. The people of Suffolk found themselves having to cope with several changes of the religion of the nation. Thus, livelihoods and lives themselves often depended on one's religious faith as much as it did on social position or wealth.

THE IPSWICH BUTCHER'S SON

By the end of the fifteenth century, Ipswich was a bustling, thriving community with numerous churches, five monastic orders and four hospitals. The town centre was packed with markets and shops offering all manner of goods. Undoubtedly, one of the most powerful men in England during the reign of King Henry VIII was Thomas Wolsey, who was born in Ipswich in the early 1470s. Although he was often described as a butcher's son, mainly by his enemies who sought to belittle the great man, Wolsey's father was probably a modest landowner who sold the livestock he reared on his land.

Thomas Wolsey benefitted from an education at Ipswich Grammar School that, coupled with his intellect and ambition, enabled him to attend Oxford University followed by a rapid rise through the ranks of the Catholic Church. In 1514, he was appointed Archbishop of York and a year later the Pope made him a cardinal. This was followed a month later by Henry VIII appointing him as Lord Chancellor of England. He therefore became the king's right-hand man. As one of the monarch's closest councillors, Thomas Wolsey became a rich man and, not forgetting his roots, he set about constructing a school for fifty boys in Ipswich, the College of St Mary, which opened in 1528. Just one year after opening, the school was such a success that Wolsey drew up ambitious plans for it to be enlarged. However, he was destined not to implement these. Cardinal Wolsey was stripped of his role of Lord Chancellor in 1529 and his property seized. His equally rapid fall from power was due to him enraging the king by not being able to secure a fast annulment for Henry of his marriage to Catherine of Aragon so that

Wolsey's Gate, Ipswich, in 1785.

the king could marry Anne Boleyn. Wolsey died a year later, and his Ipswich college was closed. Henry VIII ordered the demolition of the buildings. Only the former waterside gate, the southernmost entrance to Thomas Wolsey's college, remains today.

TUDOR CELEBRITIES IN LOVE

When it came to Tudor celebrities in Suffolk they did not come greater than Charles Brandon, Duke of Suffolk, and his wife, Mary, sister to King Henry VIII. Charles Brandon was one of the king's closest companions and when Henry's sister, Mary, became a widow shortly after her marriage to King Louis XII of France in 1515, Henry asked Brandon to return to the continent to bring his sister home. Charles Brandon and Mary already knew each other well from the royal court and the question of their marriage had been discussed in the past between Henry and Brandon. The widowed Mary was worried that Francis, the French Dauphin, or her brother the king might marry her off to someone else like Louis and so Charles and Mary were married in secret in Paris on their way back home to England. Henry was furious when he discovered their deception, although, with the help of Cardinal Wolsey, the king's anger was assuaged, and the Duke and Duchess of Suffolk settled down in their newly built country estate of Westhorpe Hall near Stowmarket.

Mary died in 1533 and records still exist that detail the arrangements for her funeral in Bury St Edmunds. The funeral procession included 100 torch bearers, clergy carrying the cross, other nobility and 100 of the Duke of Suffolk's yeomen. The coffin started its journey at Westhorpe placed on a carriage draped with black velvet and drawn by six horses trapped in black. A pall of black cloth edged with gold was placed over the coffin, upon which rested a beautiful funeral effigy of the late Queen of France in her robes of state, a golden crown on her head and a sceptre brought especially from France in her hand. Mary was originally buried in the abbey at Bury St Edmunds, although when the institution was dissolved by her brother, her remains were moved to the nearby church of St Mary's, where her tomb can be seen today.

REFORMATION AND DISSOLUTION

The English Reformation and the subsequent dissolution of the monasteries changed the face of Suffolk forever. When Henry VIII broke from the Catholic Church and declared himself Head of the Church of England, he started on a course that was to see the power shift from the church to the state. The reasons why the king decided to suppress the various religious orders are many and complex, but it is clear that he saw these Catholic institutions as centres of opposition to his break from Rome and the Pope.

There were then eighteen monasteries, eleven friaries and six nunneries in Suffolk and it was the monasteries, and some nunneries, that were the main landowners, owning great swathes of the county. Of these monasteries, the Benedictine Abbey of Bury St Edmunds was by far the largest and most powerful. Even so, it had far fewer monks – around sixty – than it had done in its heyday in the Middle Ages. The three next largest monasteries, Butley, Leiston and Ixworth, had little more than twelve monks each; a pattern not unique to Suffolk. Bury St Edmunds was also by far the wealthiest, with an annual income of £1,659 in 1535: it was the fifth wealthiest Benedictine house in England. The abbey's estates extended across the eastern counties and even to London, and it was the largest single landholder in west Suffolk apart from the Crown. The other Suffolk institutions were far less wealthy with only Butley Priory and the Cistercian abbey at Sibton having an annual income of more than £200. Between 1536 and 1539 all thirty-five of Suffolk's religious houses were closed.

The dissolution began with the smaller establishments and since there was little opposition to the closures, Henry VIII's officials pressed on with the larger establishments. All the assets from these religious houses were confiscated by the Crown. The monks and nuns, however, fared better than is widely thought. Many had negotiated pensions with the royal commissioners and went on to lead lives outside their religious communities.

Although the king certainly gifted some of the confiscated land to close allies and advisers, the vast majority of it was sold off. The Court of Augmentations, established to dispose of land formerly held by the church, had more than 200 manors in Suffolk to sell. This presented an opportunity for noble families and gentry to consolidate and to expand their holdings. Five members of the nobility were granted land; two of whom were Thomas Howard, Duke of Norfolk, who received Sibton Abbey and Butley Priory, and Charles Brandon, Duke of Suffolk, who procured large grants of Suffolk property. The vast Suffolk holdings of the Bury St Edmunds Abbey went to various wealthy gentlemen and officials such as Sir Thomas Jermyn, Nicholas Bacon, Sir Thomas Kitson, and William Clopton.

THE HEARTS AND MINDS OF THE PEOPLE

The death of Henry VIII in 1547 heralded an unsettled period in England's cultural and religious life. Henry's only legitimate son succeeded to the throne as King Edward VI. Under the terms of Henry's will, Mary, his eldest daughter and product of his first marriage to Katherine of Aragon, inherited a number of estates in Suffolk. In total, Mary held, in this county and elsewhere, thirty-two principal manors and some minor ones that were later exchanged for Framlingham Castle only a few months before her half brother's death.

In the summer of 1553, as Edward lay on his deathbed, the Duke of Northumberland led a plot to thwart Mary's claim to the throne. However, she learned of his deceit and swiftly left Hertfordshire, where she was staying at the time, and moved on through Cambridgeshire into Suffolk. There she stayed at Hengrave Hall near Bury St Edmunds and then moved onwards to Euston Hall. These were homes of Catholic families – the Kitsons and the Rookwoods – who were loyal to Mary. By the time she had moved on into Norfolk, the king's death was confirmed, and Lady Jane Grey was proclaimed queen. Mary stayed put in Norfolk, rallying friends and supporters amongst the East Anglian gentry and on 12 July, with her forces growing, Mary moved on to Framlingham, one of the strongest fortifications in the area. It was therefore an ideal place from which to defend oneself against an enemy. As she journeyed to Framlingham, many of the local gentry and justices, together with a crowd of country folk, gathered in the deer park adjacent to the castle to await her arrival. By the time Mary and her supporters received word that the Duke of Northumberland was in East Anglia and headed for the castle, an army of 500 men had been mustered to defend her. However, within days, Privy Council support for Jane had waivered and it declared Mary queen on 19 July.

As bells rang out across the country to celebrate the accession of Queen Mary, she left Framlingham to begin her triumphant progress towards London. Along the route and at her various stopping places, she received

A coin depicting Queen Mary I.

the homage of her subjects. At Ipswich she was met by the bailiffs of the town, who presented her with eleven pounds sterling in gold, and by some young boys who gave her a golden heart inscribed with the words 'The Heart of the People'. However, her five-year reign was overshadowed by her aggressive attempts to reverse the English Reformation and to return the country to Catholicism. In the process she had many religious dissenters burned at the stake, including thirty from Suffolk,

nine of whom are commemorated on the Martyrs'
Memorial in Christchurch Park in Ipswich.

REBELLION

By the sixteenth century, the Suffolk woollen cloth trade
had spread over a wide area outside its original southern
Suffolk centres and, although some clothiers were indi-
vidually wealthy, the industry suffered several serious
recessions. There was a falling demand for Suffolk dyed
cloth on the European market and export restrictions in
this country hit them hard. By comparison, agriculture
was booming. There was a growing demand for food,
fuelled by an enormous rise in population. However,
labourers' wages were not keeping pace with food prices,
resulting in increased profit margins for the food produc-
ers: the rural gentry and yeoman farmers.

Compared with previous dynasties, the Tudor reign
of England was relatively stable. Nevertheless, at
various times during the sixteenth century, Suffolk's
working-class population let off steam against the monarch and government. In 1525, against the backdrop
of the already declining cloth industry and steadily
rising prices, Suffolk textile workers were faced with
an unwelcome taxation in the form of the 'Amicable
Grant'. Henry VIII needed money to finance his war with
France and so Cardinal Wolsey ordered the implementa-
tion of this nationwide tax. Discontent quickly spread
through the country and people claimed that the tax
was unconstitutional. The largest protests were in the
south-west of Suffolk in the cloth-making region, with
Lavenham as its centre. Around 4,000 people gathered to

demonstrate against the grant but, although they out-numbered the army led by the Dukes of Suffolk and Norfolk sent to quell the uprising, the rebels were defeated. More than 500 of the ringleaders were indicted and imprisoned in London. In the end, however, Henry VIII relented and did not collect the tax, aware how much the support of his subjects mattered.

Two decades later, unrest once again swept through England, this time centred on the agricultural working population. Their main grievances were the over-use of land, especially the common land where peasants grazed their animals, and also the perceived mismanagement by landowners. Inflation, unemployment, rising rents and declining wages also added to the mix. The most serious of the unrests was in Norfolk and became known as 'Kett's Rebellion' but it soon spread to other locations in Suffolk: Bury St Edmunds and Melton. Whilst in Norfolk, military force was necessary to put down the rebels, in Suffolk influential noblemen were able to negotiate with the protesters, thus preventing any real conflict.

BLACK SHUCK

Most parts of Britain have their own version of the black dog legend and each region has a different name for the beast. However, probably the most unforgettable black dog case occurred in Suffolk and dates back to 4 August 1577 when 'a Straunge and terrible Wunder' befell the churches of St Mary's, Bungay and Blythburgh. During morning service in Bungay, an unusually violent storm was raging outside when the proceedings were disrupted by a huge black dog that burst in surrounded by lightning flashes. It swept through the building 'with greate swiftnesse and incredible haste among the people' and when it passed between two of the worshippers it 'wrung the necks of them bothe at one instant clene backward insomuch that, even at a moment where they kneeled, they straungely died'. Another unfortunate man survived but was shrivelled up 'like a piece of leather scorched in a hot fire'.

This dog, known locally as Black Shuck (from the Danish *succa* to mean the devil or evil spirits), was believed by the witnesses to this event to have been the devil in animal form. As well as its fearsome appearance, it was reported to have had a sulphurous smell, and when the places where it had been were examined, there was a smell of brimstone as well as the ground being scorched.

We know so much detail about this canine visitation because of a contemporary pamphlet written and published by Rev. Abraham Fleming, a prolific author on all sorts of subjects from earthquakes to translations of Latin classics. In *A Straunge and terrible Wunder*, Fleming also tells how, on the very same day, the Black Shuck appears some 10 miles away in Blythburgh accompanied again with a flash of lightning that struck the spire, sending tons of masonry through the roof, killing two men and a young lad. The dog also left his trademark in the form of deep, black claw marks on the north door of the church and these can still be seen today.

VISIBILITY AND HOSPITALITY

When Queen Elizabeth I acceded to the throne in 1558, she inherited a country that had suffered religious and political upheavals during the five-year reign of her half-sister, Mary. Elizabeth therefore set about promoting a feeling of unity and a sense of loyalty to their sovereign among her subjects. One of the key ways to achieve this was to be as visible as possible to as many people as she could, and the queen therefore embarked on a series of summer progresses to different parts of her realm.

In August 1561, Elizabeth visited Ipswich, staying for almost a week at Christchurch Mansion, and in the summer of 1578, she travelled through Suffolk on her way to and from Norwich. Queen Elizabeth's 1578 progress out of London took eleven weeks in total and she travelled with a supporting cast of Privy Councillors, more minor court officials, as well as servants. They rode on horseback and were accompanied by several hundred horse-drawn carts, which carried everything necessary to establish the queen's personal chambers, as well as what was required for her to continue to govern her country on the move. A contemporary account by Thomas Churchyard of the queen's reception when crossing the border from Essex into Suffolk reads:

> there were two hundred young gentlemen clad all in white velvet, and three hundred of the graver sort apparelled in black velvet coats and fair chains, all ready at one instant and place, with fifteen hundred serving men more on horseback, well and bravely mounted in good order, ready to receive the Queen's Highness into Suffolk … But before her Highness passed to Norfolk, there was in

Suffolk such sumptuous feasting and banquets, as seldom in any part of the world hath been seen before.

During her progresses, Elizabeth chose to stay at various country houses on her route. Whilst noble gentlemen were honoured at being chosen to host the queen, it presented them with a huge logistical and monetary burden. Some even risked becoming (or became) bankrupt after having to provide board, lodging and entertainment for the monarch and her entourage. In 1578 her Suffolk hosts included Sir William Cordell at Melford Hall; Sir William Drury, who held Lawshall Hall; Edward Rookwood at Euston Hall; and Sir Thomas Kitson of Hengrave Hall. Although some of the queen's hosts that summer were Protestant, others including Rookwood and Kitson followed the outlawed Catholic faith.

Hengrave Hall.

Nevertheless, it is clear that Queen Elizabeth was more interested in her comfort than in the religion of the families with whom she stayed.

A CLASSICAL EDUCATION

The latter part of the sixteenth century saw the beginning of the heyday of the grammar school. These schools were where boys were prepared for university and, although some were run by individual masters on a commercial basis, Suffolk saw a rise in charitable endowments for such institutions. These grammar schools founded by wealthy benefactors did not necessarily mean that they offered education free of charge, even though some were called 'free schools'. Often the endowment covered a certain number of free places in addition to money for the schoolmaster's salary and upkeep of the school buildings. But some grammar schools fared better than others in terms of their endowments and therefore some continued for many centuries, even to the present day, whilst others failed due to lack of funds.

Most grammar schools drew their pupils from the immediate neighbourhood, and those beyond walking or pony-riding distance would have to board. During this period the vocational purpose of the grammar school changed. With English becoming more popular, Latin was no longer a necessity for professionals and, even for the clergy, the English language was widely used in liturgy. Grammar schools, however, continued to teach Latin and Greek for those who intended to go to university, and expanded their curriculum to take in classical history, geography and mythology. Boys would start at the grammar school at the age of 7 or 8 and move on to university, if they were good enough, at 14 or 15 years of age.

In Bungay in 1580, local landowner Lionel Throckmorton gave a plot of land in Earsham Street for the erection of a new grammar school. One already existed, in the corner of the churchyard of St Mary's, but it was clearly too small for Throckmorton's plans to educate local boys. He also gifted money for the building of the school and founded scholarships for poor boys to go to Cambridge. Throckmorton's original school was burned to the ground in 1688, when much of the town was destroyed. But a replacement was quickly constructed. For many grammar schools, ordinances and rules were written, which governed the organisation and management of the institution. For Bungay, these date from 1591–92 and are extraordinarily detailed. The main criteria set out in these rules for prospective pupils were that they should already be able to read and write 'in some reasonable sort', and that they were free from any infectious disease.

At Botesdale, Nicholas Bacon, the lord of the manor of Redgrave, bought the former chantry chapel sometime after it had been dissolved under Edward VI along with similar establishments up and down the country. In 1561, Bacon obtained a charter from Queen Elizabeth I to found a grammar school in the chapel building. The chapel was used as the schoolroom and pupils were given board and lodging in a newly built, adjoining house. The comprehensive ordinances and rules were set out by Nicholas Bacon himself in 1576 a few years before he died and detail how the money he had given to keep the school running should be spent. Like Throckmorton in Bungay, Bacon made provision for scholarships to Cambridge. He specified that poor children should be given preference. He also wrote into his ordinances some rules that should be given to parents wanting to send their boy to the school, which read:

> You shall submit your child to be ordered in all things after the discretion of the schoolmaster.
>
> You shall find your child sufficient ink, paper, pens, books, candle for winter and all other things at any time requisite and necessary for the maintenance of his learning.
>
> You shall allow your child at all times a bow, three shafts, bowstrings, a shooting glove and a brace to exercise shooting.
>
> You shall see diligently from time to time that your child keep daily the ordinary hours and times in coming to school, and if he shall fail therein or be absent three days in a quarter without reasonable cause (as sickness) he shall be banished [from] the said school.

Bacon also set out reasons why the schoolmaster or usher (the schoolmaster's deputy) may be removed, either temporarily or permanently, from the school. These included having an infectious disease, being absent without leave, or committing a crime such as 'whoredom, drunkenness or perjury'.

GAME IS THE GAME

William Camden wrote the first known geographical and historical survey of Great Britain and Ireland, which was published in 1586 under the title *Britannia*. He visited East Anglia in 1578, the same year that Queen

Elizabeth I herself made a summer progress to the region. Originally written in Latin but translated into English during Camden's lifetime, *Britannia* provides us with a fascinating insight into the counties, towns and villages through the eyes of an Elizabethan gentleman. This is how he describes Suffolk generally:

> A large country it is, and full of havens, of a fat and fertile soile (unlesse it be Eastward), being compounded (as it is) of clay and marle: by meanes whereof there are in every place most rich and goodly corne fields, with pastures as battable [useful] for grazing and feeding of cattell. And great store of cheeses are there made, which to the great commodity of the inhabitants are vented into all parts of England, nay in to Germanie, France, and Spain also ... Neither be their wanting woods heere, which have beene more plentifull, and parkes, for many their are lying to Noble mens and Gentlemens houses, replenished with game.

This final reference is to deer parks on the numerous large, country estates in the county. They had fulfilled a number of roles in the medieval era: they were status symbols and places for leisure and recreation. The number of such deer parks had declined in the fifteenth century but recovered in Tudor times as new, wealthy landowners drawn from trading and legal backgrounds invested in country estates. Sir Thomas Elyot, writing at the time, talks at some length on the subject. Well-bred young boys should be skilled in hunting because it 'increaseth in them both agility and quickness, also a sleight and policy, to find such passages and straights where they may entrap their enemies'. Hunting was considered a good way of keeping fit both mentally and physically. It was also a good remedy for idleness and all the temptations that this brought with it. Wealthy young men could spend hours following the hunt.

Helmingham Hall is considered to be one of the finest Tudor houses and estates in Suffolk. Construction was started by John Tollemache in 1480 and the estate is still in the same family's hands today. Also present today are red and fallow deer, probably the descendants of deer that roamed the 400-acre park in the time of Queen Elizabeth I. The monarch, who was renowned for 'dropping in' on landed gentry, visited Helmingham twice. It is therefore highly likely that she found time during her visits to take the opportunity to go deer hunting, one of her favourite pastimes.

CARRY ON CAMPING

A popular game enjoyed by the working classes in Elizabethan England, especially in the eastern counties, was football, which at the time had more in common with our modern rugby than soccer. The earliest reference found so far for a Suffolk game is in Hollesley in 1320, when four pairs of men were 'involved in bloody assaults' while 'playing'. Often known as 'camping' or 'camp-ball' in the Tudor era, football was a far more violent game than its later incarnation. Sir Thomas Elyot dismisses it at as nothing but 'beastly fury and extreme violence whereof proceedeth hurt and consequently rancour and malice do remain with them that be wounded'. Another writer on the subject, the Puritan Philip Stubbes, was of a like mind, declaring that camping:

May rather be called a friendly kind of fight than a play or recreation; a bloody murdering practice than a fellowly sport or pastime for does not everyone lie in wait for his adversary seeking to overthrow him and to pitch him on his nose, though it be upon hard stones, in ditch or dale, in valley or hill or whatsoever place it be he careth not, so he have him down ... By this means sometimes their necks are broken, sometimes their backs, sometimes their legs, sometimes their arms, sometimes their noses gush out with blood, sometimes their eyes start out ... And no marvel, for they have sleights to meet one betwixt two, to dash him against the heart with their elbows, to hit him under the short ribs with their gripped fists and with their knees to catch him up on the hip, and to pitch him upon his neck ... Is this murdering play now an exercise for the Sabbath day?

Games of camp-ball were often played on a Sunday after church, with the opposing sides coming from neighbouring villages. Indeed, many parishes designated a special site for communal recreation often called a Camping Close. It was a grass field, less than 4 acres in size enclosed by hedges and ditches. Many places in Suffolk can still identify the place where this game was played, as the field name was often used on maps long after the game had ceased to be played there. We therefore see names such as such as 'Camping Close' in Eye, the 'Camping Pightle' in Hawstead and 'Camping Land' in Stowmarket.

THE WELFARE STATE

The dissolution of the monasteries by Henry VIII signalled the end, albeit temporarily, of much of the help to the poor and infirm. Abbeys, including the one at Bury

St Edmunds, had established hospitals not necessarily to tend to the sick but to look after those people who were unable to look after themselves through lack of work and often disability or old age. The largest of the six hospitals in Bury St Edmunds was St Saviour's. As well as providing food and shelter for pilgrims visiting the abbey, it housed twelve poor men and twelve poor women. When the abbey was closed in 1539, the hospital went too. However, it was not long before wealthy individuals endowed similar institutions called almshouses, aimed at looking after the needy in Elizabethan society, often the elderly. These benefactors were motivated by a promise of a reward in heaven and, of course, their name living on in their foundations. The donors often stipulated the number of places to be provided

The Hospital of the Holy Blessed Trinity, Long Melford.

in the almshouses as well as other criteria to be met by those individuals.

In 1587, a rich landowner called Thomas Seckford was granted a licence by Queen Elizabeth I to build and endow almshouses in Woodbridge 'to relieve need and distress' in the community. The building was to be occupied by twelve men and a principal almsman and prospective occupants needed to demonstrate that they had lived 'honestly' in the town for at least three years. The almsmen were mostly skilled or semi-skilled workers around the age of sixty and received an annual pension of £5 on top of their board and lodging. In return, the men had to follow a strict regime that included not drinking alcohol. They also had to attend church three times a week. The Hospital of the Holy Blessed Trinity in Long Melford was founded in 1573 by the lord of the manor of Melford, Sir William Cordell. The almshouses stand next to the parish church and originally housed twelve 'brethren' who were local poor men. Cordell endowed the institution with land and property in the surrounding area to ensure a regular source of income. Such Elizabethan foundations paved the way for many more almshouse buildings, some grand like these but many more were modest units of accommodation that continue to the present day.

POTHOLES

From the last years of the reign of Queen Elizabeth I at the beginning of the seventeenth century, to the eve of the accession of Queen Victoria in the mid-1830s, there were four key posts in every parish in England and

Wales. Between them they had responsibility for the various services and duties that the parish was obliged by
law to exercise, working alongside, and in consultation
with, the ratepayers. These officials were, in order of
precedence, the churchwarden, the overseer of the poor,
the surveyor of the highway, and the constable. In carrying out their various tasks these officials ensured, as best
they could, that the community enjoyed good government. Overall it was a remarkably effective system. After
all, it lasted with relatively few changes for some 250
years. It was built on the basis of local responsibilities
that went back several more centuries to the period after
the Norman Conquest. The parish had a high degree of
autonomy and control of its own affairs. And it was not
until the interventionist nineteenth century that central
government seriously began to concern itself with the
detail of how a local community worked.

The surviving documents created by Suffolk's parish
officers are largely kept by the county's archive service.
These records give an invaluable insight into how the
county's towns and villages were administered. To be
appointed surveyor of the highway for your parish was
unwelcome. Since 1555, parishes had been responsible
for the upkeep of roads and bridges within their own
boundary. All able-bodied males had to undertake compulsory highway labour for a certain number of days
each year, and it was the job of the surveyor to ensure
that they did. Like the other parish officials, surveyors of
the highway kept account books detailing payments for
materials and labour. Most of these accounts show that
for the majority of the time, the official was paying out
money to those who brought stones from their land with
which the potholes in the road were filled. Clearly, then,

potholes are not just a modern problem as can be seen in this account written by the Shakespearean actor Will Kemp, who danced a morris from London to Norwich, passing through the Suffolk countryside:

This foul way I could find no ease in, thick woods being on either side the lane, the lane likewise being full of deep holes. In this foul way two pretty plain youths watched me and with their kindness somewhat hindered me. One, a fine light fellow, would be still before me, the other at my heels. My youth that followed me took his jump and stuck fast in the midst crying out to his companion – 'come George, call ye this dancing!' Indeed he could go no further till his fellow was fain to wade and help him out. I could not choose but laugh to see how like two frogs they laboured.

5

STUART SUFFOLK

The House of Stuart reign over the country can be described simply as a period of war and turmoil. From the 1630s onwards, life in Suffolk became increasingly perilous and turbulent. Frequent outbreaks of the plague (albeit not as devastating as in the fourteenth century) hit the workforce and general morale hard. The woollen industry, upon which Suffolk had relied for much of its economic well-being, was already depressed by the time the first Civil War broke out in 1642. Although the county was less affected, and involved, than many others throughout this and the second Civil War, from 1648 to 1649, Suffolk suffered under the subsequent Puritan parliamentary rule until the Restoration in 1660. Even after this, because of its strategic coastal position, the county became embroiled in the three separate wars Britain fought against the Dutch.

On the religious front, Suffolk both prospered and endured persecution in equal measure. It was a county with a real fervour for nonconformism, often in the forefront of new forms of congregation. This meant, however, that nonconformists and their ministers suffered hardship and physical punishment because of their faith. It was not until the end of the seventeenth century that toleration of nonconformists allowed all forms of religion in Suffolk to flourish.

IPSWICH, MASSACHUSETTS

Suffolk rightly claims to have been the home of many of the founding fathers of the United States of America. One of the now recognised unsung pioneers from the county was Captain Bartholomew Gosnold. Gosnold was born in Grundisburgh in 1571 and his family seat was nearby at Otley Hall. He captained two expeditions to the New World. The first was in 1602 when he founded and named Cape Cod, Martha's Vineyard (named after his daughter) and Cutty Hunk. The second was in 1607 when he was the prime mover in the formation of the first English-speaking colony in Jamestown (in what is now known as Virginia). Gosnold died only four months after landing in America for the second time.

Around 650 people from Suffolk emigrated to New England, most during the 1630s. This was a difficult time for the county with the woollen industry in deep depression and outbreaks of the plague. It was also a time of social, religious and political turmoil. Suffolk had many Puritans who were at odds with the established Church of England and the government of King Charles I. For many, therefore, the promise and hope of a new life across the Atlantic where they could set up a new church was a key attraction. This was on top of their dissatisfaction with the situation at home. Suffolk yeomen, husbandmen and craftsmen joined clergy and gentlemen in selling their homes and possessions and took their families to the New World to start a new life.

John Winthrop was born at Groton Manor near Sudbury in 1587. Like many other Puritans, he emigrated to America in 1629. There he founded the city of Boston and was the second governor of Massachusetts. Winthrop also founded the town of Ipswich, Massachusetts in 1634 which is one of a number of places in the United States with Suffolk place names. Others include Sudbury, founded in the 1630s, and Haverhill, again in Massachusetts, where many of the first British immigrants settled. Framingham (without the 'l') was named for Framlingham after the death in 1700 of Suffolk man Thomas Danforth, a Bay Colony official who had settled in the new town.

NEUTRAL SUFFOLK

Although it certainly cannot be said that Suffolk was unaffected by the turbulent period of the English Civil Wars and the subsequent Commonwealth under Oliver Cromwell, the county was far less engaged in the conflict than many others. Of the gentry – the principal landowners – in Suffolk at that time, only about a quarter participated in the wars. Thus, the remainder – around 500 – were neutral, neither needing nor wanting to take sides between the Royalists and Parliamentarians. As a result, the county saw no serious fighting. In March 1643, the only military event was the so-called Siege of Lowestoft, which lasted no more than an hour during which Royalist gentry took control of the town. Cromwell and his troops swiftly rode into

Lowestoft, surprised the opposition and took the town without a fight.

From the outbreak of the first Civil War, through to the Restoration of the monarchy in 1660, Suffolk was governed by an unpaid committee that met regularly in Bury St Edmunds. On the committee were the heads of the principal landowning families in the county, such as Sir William Spring of Pakenham and Sir John Rous of Henham. The wealthiest man in Suffolk was Sir Nathaniel Barnardiston of Kedington. He led the group whose main job it was to raise troops, horses and money for the Parliamentarians. This filtered down into similar activity at parish level. For instance, in March 1643 the village of Shimpling provided five volunteers for the Eastern Association (a purely defensive alliance of eastern counties) as well as collecting money and arms. The latter comprised a sword, seven muskets and an old helmet!

During this period, the Puritan parliament outlawed any ritual or religious celebrations, including Christmas and Easter. Another casualty of this was May Day, where the tradition of erecting and dancing around a maypole was banned. However, in 1647 a group of around 200 Bury St Edmunds townspeople led by Colonel Blague, a staunch Royalist, rebelled against this ruling. They put up a maypole in the market square and prepared to dance. The town elders, in an attempt to uphold the law, ordered that it be taken down. A riot ensued, and Cromwell's New Model Army of Roundheads were called to deal with the demonstrators.

DISSENTERS

Suffolk has a long history of Protestant nonconformity. Such dissenters first appeared in the fourteenth century, when the so-called Lollards followed the teachings of John Wycliffe. After the English Reformation, there were also breakaway groups who had differences of opinion from the mainstream Church of England. After about 1600, nonconformity grew rapidly. During the Civil Wars, however, with the Puritans in control of the government, many different types of nonconformist places of worship sprung up. In 1651 in Suffolk, all the main dissenting congregations were represented including the Methodists, Wesleyans, Primitive Methodists, Independents, Congregationalists, Baptists, Presbyterians, Unitarians and the Quakers. In March 1644, an official anti-Puritan purge was instigated in Suffolk. As a result of evidence given by their own parishioners, which clearly varied in authenticity, about 100 incumbent ministers were ejected from their Suffolk parishes. For instance, the rector of Playford, Lionel Payters, was accused of 'eating custard after a scandalous manner' and of offering his crop of hemp 'to hang up the Roundheads'.

The two most important denominations in this county were the Quakers, who saw no need of a ministry between the believer and God, and the Independents (or Congregationalists) who believed that each congregation should be self-governing. The seventeenth century saw several periods during which nonconformists were persecuted for their faith. Quakers, who seemingly presented both a religious and social threat, were treated particularly harshly. In 1657, a Quaker preacher called George Whitehead was ordered to be whipped at Nayland 'till his body be bloody'. Two years later, George Fox of Charsfield was first imprisoned for preaching in the market in Aldeburgh and later incarcerated for preaching in a church in Southwold. However, in 1672, King Charles II allowed official licensing of nonconformist ministers and places of worship (usually private houses). We know, therefore, that there were at least ninety-eight towns and villages in Suffolk that contained nonconformist congregations at that time, with twenty-seven having more than one. Quaker meetings, however, were not licensed and by nature of their organisation, a monthly meeting would rotate among several venues. However, we do know that there were forty-two Quaker meetings in the county in the 1670s.

Final recognition of religious dissenters came in 1689 with the Toleration Act under King William III and

Walpole Old Chapel.

Queen Mary II. This is when many purpose-built chapels were erected by various denominations. On 19 August 1689, Halesworth's Independent congregation were granted the lease of a sixteenth-century farmhouse in Walpole at an annual rent of ten shillings. The farmhouse was transformed into a dramatically large, full-height room with box pews downstairs and a tiered gallery above on three sides of the building, all facing a hexagonal canopied pulpit from which the minister would conduct the service. Today, it is one of the oldest, surviving nonconformist chapels in England and although it is now formally closed, it continued as a regular place of worship through to 1970.

THE MAN WHO DESTROYED ANGELS

By the seventeenth century, Suffolk's parish churches had already undergone a drastic transformation. They had survived the destruction of devotional images at the time of the English Reformation: interior walls had been whitewashed to cover up fabulous wall paintings of biblical scenes, rood screens with colourful images of the saints had been taken down or dismantled, and statues had been crushed. But many fine architectural features and rich fittings had remained. However, the English Civil Wars together with the Puritan movement brought a further crushing blow to these churches. The Puritans asserted that the Church of England had only been partially reformed in the sixteenth century and they sought to purify the Church from all its remaining 'Catholic' practices. Therefore, in 1641 the Puritan Parliament enacted an ordinance that stated 'all monuments of superstition and idolatry should be removed and abolished', targeting specifically: 'fixed altars, altar rails, chancel steps, crucifixes, crosses, images of the Virgin Mary and pictures of saints or superstitious inscriptions'.

William Dowsing was a Suffolk man, born in Laxfield in 1596. As a Puritan, he served in the armies of the Eastern Association, responsible for supplies and administration. In December 1643, he was appointed 'Commissioner for the destruction of monuments of idolatry and superstition' and, along with others charged with the same role across the country, he was responsible for destroying or ordering the destruction of any church fittings or architectural items that were considered religious icons. What made Dowsing infamous, however, was that, unlike his fellow commissioners, he kept a journal recording much of what he did in shocking detail. William Dowsing carried out his work in late 1643 and 1644, visiting more than 150 Suffolk churches, accompanied by his assistants, who acted as enforcers. One of the first churches in the county he visited was Clare where, according to Dowsing's own journal:

> We brake down a 1000 pictures superstitious; and brake down 200, 3 of God the Father, and 3 of Christ, and the Holy Lamb, and 3 of the Holy Ghost like a dove with wings; and the 12 Apostles were carved in wood, on the top of the roof, which we gave order have taken down; and 20 cherubims to be taken down.

In May 1644, the scope of the ordinance was widened to include representations of 'angels, rood lofts, holy water stoups, and images in stone, wood and glass and on plate' and since Dowsing had a particular hatred of angels, he caused many of the stunningly beautiful angel roofs to be destroyed. Angels were either taken down altogether or they were defaced, although some escaped destruction. On his visit to the church at Blythburgh, William Dowsing recorded that:

> There were 20 superstitious pictures; on the outside of the church 2 crosses one on the porch and another on the steeple; and 20 cherubims to be taken down in the church and chancel.

However, the Commissioner left before witnessing the destruction and the people of Blythburgh chose not to comply with this order. Thus, this magnificent angel roof remains intact.

An angel on the roof of Holy Trinity Church, Blythburgh.

THE WITCHFINDER GENERAL

The dust created by the widespread destruction of religious icons had not even settled when Suffolk was hit by a secular purge, fuelled by centuries of superstition. The fear of witchcraft and magic was – and is – a natural human reaction against the unknown, and the alleged perpetrators of such deeds were regarded with a high degree of mistrust. Therefore, persecution of so-called witches had appeared in Elizabethan times and continued throughout the seventeenth century. This reached a peak in East Anglia due to the actions of self-titled Witchfinder General Matthew Hopkins. Hopkins was a Suffolk-born shipping clerk who took it upon himself to fuel the suspicions and prejudice of some people in a community against an unfortunate individual, often a poor, elderly woman who looked and acted unlike others. At the height of his notoriety, between 1645 and 1647, Hopkins toured the eastern region extorting confessions from suspects by torture.

More than half the 202 people in eastern England accused of, and subsequently hanged for, witchcraft because of Hopkins' intervention were in Suffolk. Many of these were tried at the August 1645 Assizes in Bury St Edmunds and a surviving, published pamphlet tells the tragic tale of eighteen people who were tried, convicted and hanged on 17 August. They included Susan Marchant of Hintlesham, who had confessed to making a neighbour's sow lame and having consorted with the devil. A husband and wife from Halesworth, Thomas and Mary Everard, were charged with killing people by 'both being employed in a brewhouse at Halesworth, freely confessed that they had bewitched the beer'. However, the most famous of the August 1645 victims was Rev. John Lowes, the 80-year-old Rector of Brandeston. Lowes had reportedly antagonised his parishioners so much that they were persuaded by Hopkins that their priest was a witch.

Following Hopkins' death in 1647, the persecution of suspected witches continued, most notably in 1662 when two elderly widows, Rose Cullender and Amy Denny, were accused of a whole host of malevolent, magical occurrences. These included making children cough up pins and nails, making toads explode and restoring a lame child to health. The two women were tried in Bury St Edmunds, found guilty and duly hanged. After the reign of Charles II, although witches were still feared and occasionally punished, they were no longer put to death.

AT WAR WITH THE DUTCH

Between 1651 and 1674, England fought a series of three wars with Holland, comprising many sea battles. The main areas of dispute were trade and fisheries. Since the Suffolk coastline is the closest point on the British main-land to the Dutch coast, Suffolk bore the brunt of the conflicts. In June 1665, soon after the outbreak of the second Dutch War, the coastal waters off Lowestoft were the scene of a fierce naval battle. The English side, led by the Duke of York, the brother of King Charles II, and the Dutch side were reasonably equally matched in terms of ships and firepower. Nevertheless, the English fleet were victorious, capturing or sinking thirty-two Dutch ships and losing only two themselves.

Landguard Fort in Felixstowe held a key defensive position overlooking the mouth of the River Stour opposite the Essex port of Harwich. It was the second fort to have been built on the site after the original, smaller one built by Henry VIII had fallen into disrepair. In 1666, it had been strengthened with an outer brick wall and just a year later these added defences contributed to the defeat of a brazen attempt by the Dutch to invade the English mainland; the last time such an invasion by foreign troops has been attempted to date. The Dutch goal was Harwich, although to take the town they first had to take Landguard Fort. Up to 2,000 troops landed on the beaches of Felixstowe and made efforts to scale the fort's walls armed with hand grenades and muskets. Surprised

Landguard Fort.

by the strength of the fort's garrison, the Dutch finally withdrew under cover of darkness.

In 1672, the residents of Southwold witnessed a violent sea battle that became known as the Battle of Sole Bay. The English fleet stationed along the east coast had their headquarters in Southwold under the command of the Duke of York and the Earl of Sandwich. On the morning of 28 May the Dutch fleet appeared on the horizon and English ships were launched to defend the coast. The resulting maritime battle lasted the whole day, with heavy losses sustained on both sides. Lord Sandwich's flagship was one of the casualties and its commander was drowned. The people of Southwold helped tend to the injuries of some 800 sailors. The townspeople were also paid one shilling for each dead sailor washed up on the shore that they were willing to recover and bury.

RESTORATION

The Restoration of King Charles II to the throne in 1660 brought a significant shift towards the emphasis on secular, rather than sacred, aspects of Suffolk life. There was renewed interest in improvements in agriculture and estate management. Commerce and transport also became more prominent in residents' minds, taking the place of the pre-Restoration, religious Puritanism. Nevertheless, religion and politics were still inextricably linked, and it was the political leanings of Suffolk landholders – the gentry – that shaped the county in the late seventeenth century and on into the eighteenth century. At first, the Whigs (a political party advocating parliamentary supremacy) seemed to have the upper hand in the county under the leadership of Sir Samuel Barnardiston of Brightwell Hall. The Whigs tended to be the wealthiest landowners, were low-church Anglicans and tolerated nonconformist religions. Later, though, this influence was overturned by two prominent Tories, Sir Robert Danvers of Rushbrooke and Sir Thomas Hanmer of Mildenhall.

Part of the reorganisation of revenue following the Restoration of the monarchy involved the introduction of a Hearth Tax. The first collection was in 1662 and it was abolished on the accession of William and Mary in 1689. The tax was based on the number of chimneys a property had, the very smallest and poorest properties being exempt. The surviving assessments therefore give us a complete picture of Suffolk wealth during this period. In 1674, 453 houses had ten or more hearths with eighteen of these having thirty or more chimneys. At the top of the list was Hengrave Hall, home of the Gage family, which had fifty-one hearths. This was followed by Melford Hall, held by the Cordells, and Brome Hall, home to the Cornwallis family. Ninety-five other houses had between fifteen and thirty hearths. Most of these large country houses were older residences built in or before the Tudor period. Not unsurprisingly, very little house building had taken place during the Civil Wars, although earlier in the seventeenth century new-builds had included Flixton Hall, Barningham Hall and Letheringham Abbey. Two notable houses were constructed shortly after the Restoration. Sir Samuel Barnardiston built Brightwell Hall and Sir Henry Bennet, Earl of Arlington and Secretary of State to Charles II, bought the existing Euston Hall property and extensively enlarged it. There he put on lavish entertainments, including when the monarch himself visited, during which time 200 guests were entertained for fifteen days. The diarist John Evelyn recorded the occasion:

> Came all the great men from Newmarket and other parts both of Suffolk and Norfolk, to make their court, the whole house filled from one end to the other with lords, ladies and gallants.

DRUNK IN CHARGE OF A COUNTRY

Charles II stayed at Saxham Hall near Bury St Edmunds on at least four occasions and it appears that a good time was had by all. During one of the visits, Lord Arlington, a member of the King's Privy Council who travelled with the monarch, wrote, 'I could not speak to the king at Saxham, nor until today, by reason of the uncertainty of his motions.' And the famous diarist Samuel Pepys also accompanied the king there in 1668, recording after the event:

> That the King was drunk at Saxam ... the night that my Lord Arlington come thither, and would not give him audience, or could not which is true, for it was the night that I was there, and saw the King go up to his chamber, and was told that the King had been drinking. He tells me, too, that the Duke of York did the next day chide Bab. May for his occasioning the King's giving himself up to these gentlemen, to the neglecting of my Lord Arlington: to which he answered merrily, that, by God, there was no man in England that had heads to lose, durst do what they do, every day, with the King, and asked the Duke of York's pardon: which is a sign of a mad world. God bless us out of it!

Indeed, in Pepys' original diary manuscript, there are several blank pages with no entries between 29 September and 11 October 1668, some think because there was so much drunkenness and debauchery during the visit that Pepys could not bring himself to record it. More likely, though, that the diarist had been visiting family in the neighbourhood. Pepys was also present in April 1670, when he records that King Charles was entertained at Lord Crofts' on the Saturday evening and attended a service at Little Saxham church the next day. Whether it was the tedium of the lengthy sermon or the effects of the excess alcohol from the previous night (or perhaps both!), it is rumoured that the king nodded off, subsequently having to ask for it to be printed.

THE ECONOMIC TOURIST

Celia Fiennes was born in 1662 near Salisbury, the daughter of a colonel in Cromwell's army. She began her travels around England on horseback for the sake of her health, 'by variety and change of air and exercise', visiting various spa towns up and down the country. Celia was accompanied on some journeys by her mother or her sister, though for her longest journeys she took only servants. Her journal provides a vivid portrait of a still largely unenclosed countryside with few and primitive roads, although signposts were appearing. She describes these as: 'posts and hands pointing to each road with the names of the great towns or market towns that it leads to'. Celia sought out new buildings, and new developments in agriculture and industry that would promote the prosperity of the country.

On her travels, Fiennes saw many of the finest baroque English country houses while they were still under construction. Contrary to the widespread conception that the visiting of stately homes began after the Second World War, they have been accessible to travellers of good social standing since Fiennes' time if not earlier, and her comments are one of the most interesting contemporary sources of information about them. Essentially, Celia anticipated the genre of 'economic tourism', which became a staple of travel writing throughout the next two centuries.

Celia Fiennes toured the eastern counties of England in 1698. Whilst she complimented Bury St Edmunds on its pleasing situation, she was less impressed by prices of goods. She records of Bury, 'So much company living in the town makes provision scarce and dear. However, it is a good excuse to raise the reckoning on strangers.' She also had a mixed view of Ipswich:

> This is a very clean town and much bigger than Colchester is now. Ipswich has 12 churches, their streets of a good size well pitched with small stones. Their market cross has good carving, the figure of justice carved and gilt. There are but 3 or 4 good houses in the town. The rest is much like the Colchester buildings, but it seems more shattered, and indeed the town looks a little disregarded, and by enquiry found it to be through pride and sloth.

After Ipswich, Fiennes took the road up to Beccles via Wickham Market and Saxmundham. Travelling between these two towns, she records:

> Thence to Saxmundham 8 miles more: this is a pretty big market town. The ways are pretty deep, mostly lanes very little commons.

I passed by several gentlemen's seats, one, Mr Dormer's which stands in a fine park. The entrance from the road through rows of trees discovered the front and building very finely to view, being built with stone and brick and many sashes: Looks like a new house with the open iron bar gates between pillars of stone the breadth of the house.

Before crossing the border into Norfolk, Celia Fiennes comments on Beccles and, as she does in other places on her tour, she describes the nonconformist meeting house (as she was of the same persuasion) in addition to other town features:

To Beccles is 8 miles more which in all was 36 miles from Ipswich, but exceeding long miles. This is a little market town but it is the third biggest town in the County of Suffolk. Here was a good big meeting place at least 400 hearers and they have a very good minister one Mr Killinghall; he is but a young man but seemed very serious. I was there the Lord's day. Sir Robert Rich is a great supporter of them and contributed to building the meeting place which is very neat. He has a good house at the end of the town with fine gardens. There are no good buildings in the town, being old timber and plaster work except his and one or two more. There is a pretty big market cross, and a great market kept. There is a handsome stone built Church.

FIRE!

Many of the large towns, as well as the villages, in Suffolk have suffered several devastating fires in their history. In April 1608, a conflagration in Bury St Edmunds consumed 160 houses and 140 outbuildings, with damage totalling £60,000. We know some extraordinary details about this fire because of this contemporary account written and published shortly after the tragedy. This extract tells us where the fire started and where it spread:

> It happened on Monday the tenth of April between 8 and 9 of the clock in the morning, without the east gate of the same town, in a place called Eastgate Street in the house of one Randall, a maltster. And notwithstanding that at first it began half a mile from the market place, yet was it carried thither by the violence of the wind.

It continues:

> The very market place, that was the beauty and ornament of the whole town, was the principal and chiefest part that felt the fury of this fiery assault. That place that before was had in such admiration for the goodly houses and the manner of their stately buildings, was by this untimely accident utterly defaced and made a rude continent of heaps of stones and pieces of timber, that but newly fell from those late burnt houses. The warehouses and callers about the market place, wherein were great store of fish, salt, sugar, spices and many other commodities of great value, were by this fire all turned into ashes.

The fire reportedly raged for three days, during which time fire breaks were created by pulling down houses.

In June 1667 a great fire destroyed almost all of Haverhill, including major buildings such as the almshouses, the Guildhall, the Town House and the vicarage along with all the combustible parts of St Mary's Church. Bungay was also hit by a fire in March 1688. The townspeople successfully petitioned the king to issue

A contemporary printed pamphlet detailing the Bury St Edmunds fire of 1608.

a nationwide request for financial assistance. This 'brief' gives details of the devastation:

> In four hours the flames consumed the whole town except one small street and a few houses; and destroyed one of the churches, being a large and magnificent building, together with a free-school, and three alms-houses; two eminent market crosses, and the dwelling-houses of one hundred and ninety families; many brewing offices, shops, warehouses, barns, and other houses, near four hundred in number; in which most of the sufferers, through the sudden and violent rage of the flames, lost all their household stuff, stock, goods, and substance.

In 1683, more than half of Newmarket was engulfed by a terrible inferno. However, although this was clearly a tragedy for many householders and businesses, the fire was credited with saving the life of King Charles II. The king and his brother James, Duke of York, had been at the races during the day of 22 March and planned to spend the night in Newmarket. Charles was often to be found at the town's races on certain days in the racing calendar, thus an easy target for his enemies. On this particular day, a fire broke out in the evening in a stable yard near to the market place. High winds fanned the flames and before long the town was ablaze, resulting in almost half of the buildings being destroyed and the rest badly affected by smoke. Because of this fire, the entertainment planned for the king and his brother was cancelled and the royal party therefore decided to return early to London. This decision to leave Newmarket late on the 22nd rather than the following day foiled a plot to assassinate the king. About 100 men were said to have been hidden at Rye House, a manor house in Hertfordshire, and planned to ambush and kill Charles the next day when he was travelling from Newmarket to London. Later, when news of the plot became known, several arrests were made, and King Charles declared himself 'preserved' from his enemies because of the Newmarket fire.

6

GEORGIAN SUFFOLK

Suffolk in the eighteenth century was a county improving all aspects of its life and generally enjoying it. Politically, the country as a whole was remarkably stable throughout the Georgian era and, until the Napoleonic Wars between 1803 and 1815, there were no major conflicts with other countries. Suffolk people, therefore, were left to concentrate on improving their lot in life, whatever their social standing. At the upper end of society, landowners were upgrading and rebuilding their homes, as well as employing landscape designers to transform their estates. Below them, the professional classes concentrated on better educating themselves and their families, as well as enjoying a spot of social climbing at dances. For the poor, moves in the early decades of the nineteenth century were aimed at helping those who were unable to help and support themselves, even though these seemed harsh.

Suffolk's infrastructure was also greatly improved in this period, and by the time Queen Victoria came to the throne in 1837, the county's road network was better maintained, and inland waterways were being used to the benefit of local industry. Rural Suffolk, too, saw the beginnings of change, with leading advocates of new farming techniques influencing the way in which local farmers tended their livestock and used their land.

SUFFOLK HIGH SOCIETY

The Georgian period seemed to suit Suffolk towns. Whilst most residents were unable to rebuild their houses in the latest architectural fashion, instead they changed the appearance of their old timber-framed buildings by giving them a new-style Georgian façade in brick or plaster and fitting smart sash windows. The county's market towns also took a new pride in their appearance. Beccles was noted for its well-paved streets and Woodbridge for its cleanliness. Inns in towns on major routes such as Newmarket and Saxmundham were improved as coaching houses, bringing in a steady trade.

The two main towns in Suffolk saw significant changes. When the author and travel writer Daniel Defoe visited Ipswich in the early 1700s, he was clearly impressed, as he lists several things to recommend the town including: 'Good houses at very easy rents; an airy, clean, and well-governed town; very agreeable and improving company almost of every kind; and a wonderful plenty of all manner of provisions, whether flesh or fish, and very good of the kind.' At the time of Defoe's comments, Ipswich was still trying to recover from a serious economic decline having lost its cloth manufacturing, its coal trade and most of its shipbuilding business. In the eighteenth century, however, the town shared in the expansion of regional agriculture and became a major centre of the corn trade. With the increased prosperity, though, came the desire to get rid of the old medieval walls and gates, which were seen as a nuisance to traffic and to health. The local government, therefore, demolished Ipswich's west and north gates in 1781 and 1794.

In the eighteenth century, Bury St Edmunds underwent an even more dramatic transformation than Ipswich. Whilst the town's spinning and weaving industries were waning, Bury was, instead, becoming a major social capital. Defoe said of it: 'It is a town famed for its pleasant situation and wholesome air, the Montpelier of Suffolk, and perhaps of England.' The town's commercial and professional services grew as upper classes flocked to Bury. As Defoe put it: 'the beauty of this town consists in the number of gentry who dwell in and near it, the polite conversation among them, the affluence and plenty they live in'.

The Bury Fair, held on Angel Hill each late September and early October, saw traders descend on the town to set up their sales booths, which attracted the highest levels of society. Daniel Defoe commented: 'there were, indeed, abundance of the finest ladies, or as fine as any in Britain'. Apart from the trade, there were numerous balls, plays and other cultural events. A number of these took place in the Assembly Rooms (now called the Athenaeum) which still stands on Angel Hill. The *Bury Post* published comments such as: 'Our fair is expected to be exceeding brilliant, most of the private lodgings in town being already taken by persons of the first fashion and consequence'.

By the beginning of the 1800s, though, the Bury Fair was getting a mixed reception. *The Times* on 21 October 1808 reported positively:

> The Bury fair, during last week, was honoured with more than the usual fashionable assemblage of company; comprising nearly all the most distinguished families in Suffolk and the neighbouring counties. The new Assembly Rooms exhibited, on Friday evening, a spectacle scarcely to be surpassed, there being 387 persons present, among whom the female part, for youth, beauty and elegance ... The Theatre, on the preceding and following evening, was also scarcely less fashionably attended, particularly on the latter night, when the whole of the pit was laid into boxes.

However, the commercial aspects had sadly become little more than a fun fair with sideshows popular at the time such as wild animals and human giants, dwarfs and bearded ladies. The local police began to have to turn out in force to deal with pickpockets and other petty crime. In 1865–66, a petition, with 227 names, was compiled which demanded the abolition of the fair and in 1871 the Bury Fair was held for the last time.

TURNPIKES AND TOLLS

By the beginning of the eighteenth century, Suffolk had important road links with London used by carriers of goods and passengers. The general conditions of the roads, however, remained poor and hampered further expansion of the network of highways. Therefore, the creation of a network of well-maintained roads was one of the major achievements of eighteenth-century England. This road system was not planned centrally but resulted from local enterprise, regulated through Acts of Parliament. Bodies of local trustees were given powers to levy tolls on the users of a specified stretch of road, generally around 20 miles in length. Using money received from the tolls, the trust improved and maintained a particular stretch of turnpike road. The first turnpike trust in Suffolk was authorised in 1711–12 and covered the road from Ipswich to Scole (a village on the Norfolk–Suffolk border). Eventually, fourteen separate trusts were set up in Suffolk, in total administering around 282 miles of roads. As the condition of the main routes improved, a network of stagecoach services was built up. Royal Mail coaches were introduced in 1784 and by 1836 three routes crossed through Suffolk: London to Norwich via Newmarket and Bury St Edmunds; London to Norwich via Ipswich; and London to Yarmouth via Ipswich and Lowestoft.

The turnpike trusts erected gates across the road at strategic points to collect tolls from travellers from outside the parish. The tollgates were often built at points where it was least likely that vehicle or horse users could evade payment, for instance at bridges or crossroads. Small tollhouses were built next to the gates for the toll collectors to live in. In time, tollhouses started to develop a particular style. The classic design of a tollhouse with a polygonal bay front dates from the 1820s, when turnpike roads and the coach traffic they carried were at their peak. On the major roads grand castellated houses were constructed at considerable expense to impress the wealthy travellers and influence their selection of one route over another. One of Suffolk's best-known

The tollhouse at Sicklesmere.

tollhouses is in Sicklesmere, south of Bury St Edmunds.
This double-storey house shows clearly how the shape
of the building was dictated by its original use. The windows on either side of the front door enabled the toll
collector to see any travellers coming down the road in
either direction, so that he could ensure he was outside
waiting for them to pay the toll due.

From 1767, milestones were compulsory on all such
roads, not only to inform travellers of direction and
distances, but to help coaches keep to schedule. The

distances were also used to calculate postal charges before the uniform postal rate was introduced in 1840. At their height, there were more than 200 milestones in Suffolk, about a half of which survive today. Stone, however, was in short supply in the region and when the lettering on the stones became worn, cast iron mileposts were made to attach to the existing stone. Many of these were manufactured in Ipswich at the ironworks of Jacob Garrett.

INLAND NAVIGATION

With the realisation that Suffolk goods and produce needed to reach their customers elsewhere in the country and abroad with the greatest of speed, there had first been moves to improve the county's natural rivers in the sixteenth century. In 1705, the River Stour was made navigable up to Sudbury and the River Blyth was opened up to Halesworth in 1761.

After a previous unsuccessful attempt, in 1719, to get an Act of Parliament passed, a new bill was introduced in 1789 that allowed the navigation of the River Gipping from Stowmarket to Ipswich, a stretch of some 16 miles. The act authorised the trustees to raise £20,300. Following the discovery of numerous errors in the original survey and poor workmanship by the first contractor (who was sacked), John Rennie was asked to carry out a fresh survey in 1791. He found that three locks had already been constructed with turf and timber, and recommended that the remainder should be brick and stone. The trustees had to seek Parliamentary approval to raise a further £15,000 to complete the work. A series of fifteen locks were constructed to cope with the total rise in river level of 90ft. The Stowmarket Navigation was opened on the 1 September 1793, but several parts were found to be poorly built, and damage caused by severe flooding in the winter of 1794 meant a lot more work (and more money) was needed to finish the job properly. Stowmarket, however, immediately benefitted from increased trade in corn and malt.

At the same time, there were also several proposals for canals in Suffolk, running from Stowmarket to Diss in Norfolk, from Bishop's Stortford in Essex to Lakenheath, and from Bury St Edmunds to the Essex coastal town of Manningtree. However, none of these schemes ever left the drawing board.

HOME IMPROVEMENTS

The social landscape of eighteenth-century Suffolk was dominated by country houses and stately homes. The country house was not simply a home. It was surrounded by parkland and gardens that provided opportunities for relaxation, riding and sports. Hodskinson's map of Suffolk, published in 1783, shows more than seventy such parks, which are clustered in the west of the county, around the two main towns of Bury St Edmunds and Ipswich, and near the coast. The aristocracy and gentry who owned these estates were investing heavily either in new buildings or in substantial improvements both to the house and gardens.

Arguably the greatest of Suffolk's Georgian mansions is Heveningham Hall near Halesworth. Sir Gerard Vanneck inherited the estate in 1777 from his father,

The rotunda of Ickworth House.

which included a modest house built in 1714. Vanneck immediately commissioned Sir Robert Taylor to rebuild the hall, incorporating the existing property. The new-build is an imposing two-and-a-half-storey mansion in the Palladian style, with a central block including eight giant Corinthian columns and two grand wings. The interior of the house was completed by James Wyatt three years later, and he also added an orangery in the grounds and lodges at the south gate. Heveningham is rivalled, though, by the rather eccentric Ickworth House near Bury St Edmunds, which was built for Frederick Hervey, the 4th Earl of Bristol, between 1795 and 1829. It was based on designs by the Italian architect Mario

Asprucci and the construction overseen by English architect brothers, Francis and Joseph Sandys. The dominant architectural feature is the central, three-storey, domed rotunda.

From about 1730, a new English style of garden design swept through the country. This abandoned formal, geometric designs, which included straight avenues of trees and squarely built brick walls. Instead, landscape designers favoured a more natural feel with winding rivers and lakes, great swathes of grassland, clumps of trees and plantations. The foremost exponent of this new movement was Lancelot 'Capability' Brown, who redesigned six Suffolk estates, including Redgrave Park, then owned by Rowland Holt. As well as the park, Brown substantially remodelled the hall itself in the new, favoured Palladian style – hiding the old red-brick Tudor house whose design had fallen out of favour. The new landscape of the park kept the ancient trees but added shelterbelts of new trees on the northern and eastern boundaries. Brown dammed the existing stream to produce a 50-acre lake with two islands. Together with a new orangery and other buildings dotted around the estate, the total cost of these improvements was £30,000; a princely sum in 1773 when the project was completed.

TAX AND TAX EVASION

While the upper classes in Suffolk were busy enjoying themselves, the government was equally busy inventing ways to benefit. Of course, the main means of achieving this was through taxation, and the Georgian era saw a myriad of taxes levied on those who lived well. Already in place was the window tax, which had been introduced in 1696. Glass was an expensive commodity, so there was usually a direct correlation between the number of windows in a house and the prosperity of the taxpayer. Those who objected to paying an extortionate amount of money simply bricked up some of their windows. On top of this, King George II introduced a glass tax, which was levied at a certain rate according to the weight of the glass. Manufacturers responded, therefore, by producing smaller, more highly decorated objects, often with hollow stems. One of the most imaginative of taxes, which started in 1795, was a tax on the hair powder applied to wigs. In the first year, around 200,000 people were taxed this way and so the government was encouraged to raise the tax. This was obviously more than most were prepared to pay and so cropping and combing out of the hair became fashionable instead.

Suffolk gentry also suffered under the tax payable by owners of carriages, a tax on silver plate and a tax on holders of armorial bearings. Those who had a carriage where their coat of arms might be displayed paid most. Householders who employed servants found themselves taxed for these from 1777 for male servants and from 1785 for female servants. In 1780, Rev. Amayas of Beccles paid tax on one male servant, as did Mr Assey of the same town. Elsewhere, in Sproughton, the Honourable Rev. Dr Hervey also paid tax on a male servant, whereas Sir Robert Harland paid for a grand total of eight male employees.

CONTRABAND

Smuggling was one of the major crimes that occupied column space in the eighteenth-century newspapers. This illegal trade along England's coast had grown at a prodigious rate. It became a large and lucrative industry despite the penalties imposed for those who were caught in the act. This illicit dealing in perishable goods such as tea, coffee, gin and brandy came about as a direct result of the imposition of crippling taxation by successive governments desperate to fund costly wars in Europe.

It is hardly surprising that Suffolk, with its long coastline, was a major centre for smuggling. Not only did it provide numerous places along the shoreline for landing the illegal imports, it also offered excellent roads from the coast capable of taking heavy wagons laden with goods. The Roman road leading towards Stowmarket from the coast was a convenient and well-used route for contraband heading inland. Its progress was only sporadically interrupted by the customs authorities. Nevertheless, the passing carts did not go unnoticed. Earl Soham on this route was the home of William Goodwin, a surgeon. Goodwin lived at Street Farm in the second half of the eighteenth century and the early years of the nineteenth. In his notes, entitled *Miscellany of Occurrences Persons and Curiosities*, he meticulously recorded contraband passing through the village. In the summer of 1785, he noted that twenty carts had passed by in less than a week, carrying 2,500 gallons of spirits. In February of the same year, five carts carrying 600 gallons passed in just one morning.

Earl Soham was not the only village the smuggling trade touched. In Monewden, the sexton of the local church was in league with the smugglers, and in February 1790 the revenue services seized nine tubs of spirits that he had hidden behind the Ten Commandments in the church. The vicar, sexton and clerk at nearby Rishangles were also reputed to be involved in the trade. Indeed, these rumours may well have some credence because repairs to the church in the mid-nineteenth century led to the discovery under the pulpit of the remains of kegs and bottles.

PROGRESSIVE AGRICULTURE

The three main divisions of the Suffolk landscape provided the county's farmers with opportunities for different kinds of farming. The north-west of Suffolk, comprising open fields and heaths, was called the 'Fielding'. This region relied on two complementary types of farming – corn and sheep. Similarly, the largely drained marshlands of the 'Sandlings' along the south-east coast of the county was used for grazing. In the centre of the county, 'High Suffolk' was known for its dairying and mixed farming. Its dairy cows were a distinct breed, the ancestors of the modern Red Polls. These cows produced the highly praised Suffolk butter, much of which was exported to London and elsewhere, mainly through the port of Woodbridge. Indeed, Daniel Defoe in his *Tour through the Eastern Counties* published in the 1720s comments on this product, although he is far from complimentary about another dairy product. He recorded:

Woodbridge has nothing remarkable, but that it is a considerable market for butter and corn to be exported to London; for now begins that part which is ordinarily called High Suffolk, which, being a rich soil, is for a long tract of ground wholly employed in dairies, and they again famous for the best butter, and perhaps the worst cheese, in England.

On the Suffolk coast, on the marshlands and along the river valleys in the east of the county, beef cattle were a specialisation. They were driven from Scotland and northern England at the age of about 14–16 months and they thrived on the lush grasses here. Halesworth Fair in late October was particularly noted for its lean cattle.

There have been many commentators and agricultural reformers who have influenced farming practice in the country, but perhaps none greater than Arthur Young. He was born in 1741, the son of a Suffolk clergyman. On inheriting his father's Suffolk estate of Bradfield Combust in 1759, and through becoming manager of a farm in Essex, Young emerged as a tireless propagandist for agricultural improvement, constantly experimenting with new farming methods. He spent a great deal of his life travelling in this country and in France, describing changes in both agriculture and wider social and political developments. Young's *General View of the Agriculture of the County of Suffolk* was published in 1813 and provides a detailed snapshot of the state of the county's farming. One of the plants first introduced into England by Arthur Young was chicory, mainly as a food for sheep, one of Suffolk's most numerous livestock. He remarked of chicory, 'Of all the grasses, it is perhaps the most universal grown if managed and applied with attention.'

A FRENCHMAN IN SUFFOLK

We are lucky to have a fascinating European insight into life in late eighteenth-century Suffolk. An 18-year-old Frenchman, François de la Rochefoucauld, and his brother stayed for a year in Bury St Edmunds in 1784, a time when the town was considered at the height of its prosperity and a fashionable place to be and to be seen. They toured the eastern region and François recorded his observations. He wrote about almost everything from travel to the English climate in a diary he wrote for his father back in France.

François de la Rochefoucauld wrote extensively about his experiences of farming in the region:

> Agriculture is the mainspring and the end-result of a flourishing, well-peopled state ... Here agriculture is held in the highest regard, everyone is involved in it, and the ordinary farmers are not looked on, as they are in France, as an inferior class created solely to feed the rich.

He remarks on the 'depth of wisdom and justice' in Parliament having passed laws governing the labourer's day:

> All working days are fixed between six a.m. and six p.m., summer and winter: from these twelve hours, one and a half are subtracted; half an hour for breakfast and an hour for dinner ... Their wage is fixed, but depends on the district they are in ... On the farms they hire their regular workmen by the year, as in France. In the Bury neighbourhood they are paid between eight and nine guineas a year, and food, lodging etc. They have nothing to do but clothe

The Athenaeum, Bury St Edmunds.

themselves ... At harvest-time the arrangements are completely different: the farmers contract for all the hands they need and make
a bargain with them to complete the whole job. In the Bury neighbourhood they give four and half guineas to each man for cutting
and harvesting all the wheat, oats and barley.

The Frenchman also had much to say about English
culture and his rather amusing and critical account is
summed up in this passage based on his observations at
public balls such as were held at the Athenaeum in Bury
St Edmunds:

Dancing plays the smallest part in the pleasures of the English – in
general, they have no taste for this amusement ... The two sexes
dance equally badly, without the least grace, no steps, no rhythm
... The women hold themselves badly, the head hanging forward,

the arms dangling, the eyes lowered ... the men with their knees
bent; they suddenly change direction with their legs; in short their
appearance is most disagreeable as they dance.

Something de la Rochefoucauld does not comment on,
however, is the considerable effort the middle and upper
classes appear to have taken to try to educate their off-
spring in such refinements as dancing and music. But
then he may well have been incredulous at the amount
of money spent on such specialist teaching if he did not
appreciate the results!

DANCING AND DAMES

The eighteenth-century local newspapers are simply littered with advertisements for privately run academies
for young ladies and for young men. One such typical
example, published in the *Ipswich Journal* of 19 June
1742, gives details of a boarding school for young ladies
in St Clement's Street, Ipswich, run by John and Harriet
Wood. While Mrs Wood taught needlework and English,
she paid for visiting masters to educate her charges in
writing and arithmetic. Her husband was the music and
dancing master: 'For Learning to Dance, half a Guinea
Entrance, and fifteen Shillings per Quarter, and at a
Ball five Shillings ... For Learning on the Spinnet, half a
Guinea Entrance, and fifteen Shillings a Quarter, and half
a Crown per Quarter more for the Use of an Instrument,
and keeping it in order.' Mr Wood also taught dancing
as a visiting master at a number of other similar schools
in the area. No doubt he would have used as his 'bible'

The English Dancing Master, a highly successful manual published in several editions by John Playford and his successors. The title was probably just a joke because all the best dancing masters were acknowledged to be French. Playford's book contained the music and instructions on the relevant steps for more than 100 English country dances. Playford dances, however, were never dances of the country folk. They were dances of the educated society and would have been performed with a lot of fancy stepping.

Running alongside these privately run institutions were thousands of so-called dame schools. Suffolk was suffering from a particular lack of basic education for working-class children and dame schools were private, local initiatives, each run by one woman in her home, aimed at providing a basic education to children from the labouring classes. The Rev. Richard Cobbold arrived as rector of the parish of Wortham in 1824 and aside from his spiritual and pastoral duties he was a prolific writer. His most interesting, unpublished work was the various volumes of notes and observations, together with his own watercolour illustrations, of the goings-on in Wortham focused on the characters of the various residents. On his arrival in the village, Rev. Cobbold set up a Sunday school and, later, a day school for some ninety boys and girls. He was therefore quite scathing in his comments about the illiteracy of the women who ran the dame schools, characters such as Rebecca Bobby and Maria Jolly, who he wrote about in his account of Wortham 'notables'.

According to the rector, Rebecca Bobby 'did more with her eye than with her book of instruction'. She was an extremely neat and clean person who exacted the same standards from everyone who entered her house. She taught the alphabet and how to thread a needle. Cobbold derides Mrs Bobby by saying that her scholars were as learned as herself, the dame being very ignorant and, like many who taught young children, was imposing rather than enlightening. Maria Jolly was described at her marriage as a schoolmistress and so brought her desire to educate poorer children to Wortham from her home in Wetheringsett. Cobbold described Mrs Jolly as a very bad reader and a still worse writer, although one with an inflated sense of her own importance. The clergyman describes how the letters she wrote needed much deciphering. According to Cobbold, all Mrs Jolly's advice was contained in just one phrase, 'Be a good girl (or boy)'.

THE NAPOLEONIC THREAT

With an open coastline of approximately 49 miles looking out to the European mainland, Suffolk has always been vulnerable to attack. It has therefore been subject to fortifications since the late 1400s. However, none of the various defence schemes that were designed are more striking than the surviving Martello towers. The threat of invasion by Napoleon in the late eighteenth and early nineteenth century led to one of the biggest programmes of coastal defence building in the country up to this point. A string of Martello towers started to be built that stretched eastward along and up the coast from Sussex. The idea for the towers came from a defensive structure

The quatrefoil-shaped Martello tower at Slaughden.

at Mortella in Corsica that the British Navy had found to their cost was able to withstand heavy bombardment. Each structure had 24-pounder guns mounted on the flat roof and was designed to have a garrison of twenty-four gunners.

Originally, twenty such buildings were planned in Suffolk along with two large eight-gun towers. These structures were to be placed at strategic locations along the coast between Felixstowe in the south and Aldeburgh in the north. They were designed to repel Napoleon and his armies. Work began in 1809 but eventually only seventeen Martello towers were completed, with ten associated batteries. The cost of each structure ran to some £3,000. All the towers except one had three 24-pound guns. The last, at Slaughden near Aldeburgh

at the entrance to the estuary of the River Alde, was
of a unique quatrefoil design, capable of holding
four guns.

Telegraph Plantation near the village of Icklingham
was the site of a small tower that helped form a chain
of eighteen such buildings, and the only one in Suffolk,
from London to Yarmouth. It was constructed in the
early nineteenth century to improve communications
between the Admiralty in London and its fleets based on
the east coast during the Napoleonic Wars. Each relay
station – located between 7 and 10 miles apart – housed
an ingenious 'shutter' telegraph. It consisted of a large
wooden frame fixed to the roof, which had six shutters
arranged in pairs. Each shutter was mounted by means of
a central pivot. Ropes were then attached to each shutter
so that it could be turned from a closed vertical position
to an open horizontal one. Using all six shutters, therefore, there were many combinations that could be made
to create a basic code for users. The theory was that the
first shutter telegraph station in line set the shutters to
create the desired coded message and the next station
along the line would change its shutters to copy the pattern. This happened all down the line until the other end
was able to read and decipher the message. However,
there were obvious disadvantages to such a system. The
main problem encountered was poor visibility, usually
due to fog.

There was also a separate system of signal stations
on high ground along the Suffolk coast running north
to south from Gunton, Kessingland, Covehithe, Easton
Bavents, Dunwich, Aldeburgh, Felixstowe and Orford
to Bawdsey. These stations comprised tar barrels that
could be lit as an emergency signal in the event of a

night-time invasion of Napoleon's army. At Lowestoft and Woodbridge barrels were affixed to the top of the church towers. Of course, Napoleon never invaded and so these constructions, along with the Martello towers and telegraph shutter system, were never used.

SUFFOLK'S PAUPERS

The long war with France, which continued from 1792 through to 1815 with just one short break, cut off the supply of goods from the European Continent. The price of food doubled, and the Suffolk farmers took advantage of this by ploughing up pasture to grow corn instead of rearing dairy herds. However, by 1814, corn prices began to fall again with the anticipation of the end of the conflict, and less than three years later the situation was desperate. Farmers were unable to pay the rent due on land they had leased, and many farm-hands had either been laid off or had seen their wages drop by one third. A third of Suffolk's population was suddenly unemployed. Together with the county's agricultural labourers, those families whose income was from combing wool and spinning yarn found themselves out of work due to new forms of mechanisation. These industries were moving to the newly industrialised north of England.

As a result of the labour crisis, a heavy burden fell on Suffolk parishes who were responsible for supporting the poor in their community. In the year 1817–18, poor relief in the county reached a peak and averaged more than £1 per head of the population, as opposed to Lancashire where it was just a quarter of this amount.

A high level of poor relief continued until a major law was passed in 1834 comprehensively revising the 1601 Poor Law. Under the Poor Law Amendment Act, Suffolk was divided into eighteen Poor Law unions. Each union was responsible for building or adapting an existing building to serve as a workhouse. The regime in these workhouses was designed deliberately as a deterrent rather than an attraction for those who could not support themselves. Inmates were housed in basic accommodation and given minimal food. Families entering the workhouse were split up in separate male, female and juvenile quarters. The workhouse became an institution feared by most, and families would do whatever it took to keep themselves from having to enter it. However, this new system had the desired effect of reducing drastically the cost of relief of the poor: the county's overall bill reduced by over 40 per cent.

In Suffolk, some existing houses of industry were adapted and used as union workhouses, such as the building at Onehouse, which became the workhouse for Stow Union. Other unions constructed new workhouses, such as those at Wickham Market (for Plomsgate Union), in Stradbroke (for Hoxne Union) and for Thingoe Union in Bury St Edmunds. The workhouse system continued until its formal abolition in 1929 under the Local Government Act which transferred responsibility for 'public assistance' to local authorities.

ENCLOSURE

The county of Suffolk is littered with picturesque villages, each one with its own character. However, what is not immediately evident is that some of these villages went through a dramatic transformation because of local or general Parliamentary Acts passed in the late eighteenth and early nineteenth centuries. These enclosure Acts allowed for officials to create hedged or walled fields where, up to that point, the land had been either large arable open fields or common land such as greens, heaths, fens and marshes.

The north Suffolk village of Hinderclay, which borders Norfolk, is an example of a parish altered by enclosure. In one of the main streets we see that many of the houses, which clearly date from the seventeenth century or earlier, are set back from the road by a hundred metres or so. On an early map of Suffolk, dating from 1783, Hinderclay is depicted as a large common with a solitary windmill standing on it. Around the edge of this large common are dotted various houses. The common land was where the inhabitants could graze their cattle, pigs and sheep, and cut turf to fuel their fires. In 1819 all this changed for the Hinderclay community when the common was reallocated as a result of Parliamentary Enclosure. A committee of prominent local men distributed portions of this land to residents. Often, those householders with properties adjoining the common received a parcel immediately in front of their houses. Hence the existence of long, large gardens of modern-day properties in the village. Today, even the windmill is long gone, and so very few physical signs of the original layout of Hinderclay exist.

By contrast, the nearby village of Wortham is an example of a neighbourhood unaffected by enclosure. Why? Well we don't really know, as it was up to the local powers-that-were to decide to 'enclose' or not. Wortham therefore comprises a large common or commons edged by properties old and new. Horses and sheep still graze on this common land, which is used for community gatherings and celebrations. Despite the common being dissected by a modern, main road, you can catch a glimpse of what many Suffolk villages such as Hinderclay must have looked like before the enclosure movement swept through the county.

7

VICTORIAN SUFFOLK

Suffolk people both thrived and suffered in the Victorian era, depending on where they lived as much as their social class. A burgeoning population coupled with rising unemployment, chiefly in the agricultural communities, caused many problems in the nineteenth century. This was despite large numbers of people leaving the county to settle in other parts of Britain or abroad. Rapid progress in technology and innovation was a mixed blessing for Suffolk. It allowed successful industries to grow and develop, but it also meant that many manual labourers found themselves losing their jobs to machines that could work more efficiently and effectively.

The coming of the railways to the county undoubtedly led to the success of Suffolk's seaside resorts. The tourist industry in the nineteenth century was one of the fastest-growing sectors, and those working there achieved a degree of job security. Those along the coast not involved in this were reaping the rewards from the flourishing fishing trade. And so, by the end of Queen Victoria's reign, Suffolk had a far better educated and trained workforce, ready to meet the challenges of the twentieth century.

TOWN AND COUNTRY

The first half of the nineteenth century saw Suffolk's population increase by more than 50 per cent to over 335,000 in 1851. It showed, for the first time, an equal number of people living in towns and villages. From then on, towns continued to grow at the expense of the countryside and population growth generally was slower. By the end of the century the county had 380,000 residents. A great divide opened up between the quantity and quality of housing in rural areas as opposed to urban ones.

By the middle of the century, living conditions in most of Suffolk's towns were desperately overcrowded and places such as Haverhill, Ipswich, Leiston, Lowestoft, Newmarket and Stowmarket kept on growing. Outside the towns there was another divide between 'open' and 'closed' parishes. 'Closed' parishes were in the control of just one or two landowners and, although they restricted the number of labourers who were able to take up residence in the parish, some provided good-quality accommodation in estate cottages. However, other estate workers who were not so lucky had to live outside the parish and walk a fair distance to work every day. By contrast, 'open' parishes, where there were many different landholders, were not able to control the influx of labouring families and therefore these villages and towns developed rapidly, offering far inferior housing. Although new houses were being built, mainly in the towns, these were at a rate slower than the rise in population. They were also of a poor quality, having been constructed on a shoestring.

Despite the rapid growth in the county's population, many Suffolk residents were becoming increasingly mobile. Many families in rural areas were attracted to new industrial towns in Cheshire, Lancashire, and Yorkshire as well as to London, where employment could be found in a wide range of sectors and at better rates of pay than in their home county. In fact, those who were becoming a burden to the authorities were actively encouraged to migrate to elsewhere in the country. By 1891, more than 23,000 people born in Suffolk were living in the north of England and more than 50,000 in London. The British dominions of Australia and Canada also provided opportunities for work, and

The old cast-iron bridge at Stoke, Ipswich, manufactured by Ransomes.

Suffolk people took up places on government and locally assisted schemes that paid for passage to a new life across the ocean.

A BOOM TOWN

At the end of the eighteenth century, Ipswich was still roughly the same size and shape as it had been in the early 1600s. However, all this changed rapidly in the early years of Queen Victoria's reign. Work had begun on the construction of a Wet Dock in the 1830s and when it opened in February 1842, it was the second largest enclosed dock in the country with a total water area of 33 acres. Although the existing port facilities had allowed significant import of raw materials and export of manufactured goods, the silting up of the River Orwell meant that no large vessel was able to reach the quays. Therefore, the creation of this large basin and lock paved the way for the commercial and industrial success of the town.

One Ipswich company that took full advantage of the new dock was Ransomes, one of the most important iron foundries in Suffolk. The firm was established in 1789 by Robert Ransome after he had been granted a patent for a process to harden the surface of ploughshares. A further patent, granted in 1803, allowed Ransome to further improve the durability of ploughs. This proved of great importance and by the middle of the nineteenth century, Ransomes was said to be the largest manufacturer of metal goods in the country. Its products included a large range of farming machinery, cast iron goods for railways, lawn mowers and steam engines for agricultural use. The company was also instrumental in signalling the decline of the use of horses for ploughing through the invention of the steam plough.

Another major Ipswich business that benefitted from the industrial boom was the Cobbold Brewery. In 1746 Thomas Cobbold had moved his small brewery in Harwich to Ipswich, where he built the Cliff Brewery alongside the river. The family business grew rapidly in the hands of his son and grandson and included malting as well as brewing, trading corn and coal, banking and ship-owning. By the end of the nineteenth century, the Cliff Brewery was proving inadequate and so a new building, incorporating all the new brewing techniques, was commissioned. This was constructed on the site of the old one and opened in 1896. It boasted state-of-the-art machinery such as a horizontal steam engine.

The industrial success of Ipswich allowed for expansion of the town with elite, middle-class suburbs, first to the north and west and later elsewhere. In the late Victorian and Edwardian periods, more middle-class villas sprung up around Christchurch Park and a mass of more modest terraced housing appeared to the north-west and south-east. In a century, Ipswich's population had increased six-fold, from 11,000 in 1801 to 66,000 in 1901.

RIOT AND RECOVERY

Suffolk's agriculture was in a depressed state after the Napoleonic Wars. New advances in technology, therefore, may have been a blessing to farmers. However, while the invention of the threshing machine provided

A threshing machine.

opportunities for more efficient farming methods, from the agricultural labourer's viewpoint it threatened their livelihood as well as their whole way of life. These workers, of course, lacked the crucial knowledge and skills to operate advanced machinery. *The Bury and Norwich Post* of 27 November 1811 reports:

There has not been any recent invention by which human calamity has been produced as by the new implement called the threshing machine and this in greater measure arises from unskillfulness of those employed to work it. We notice that Mr Arthur Brooks of Horringer had a very narrow escape within the last few days as the whole of his clothes, even his shirt was torn from his back and had not his men stopped the machine with such promptitude there would have been loss of limbs and probably his life.

Many, however, were not so lucky and there were also reports of maiming and accidental death of labourers, some caused by mixing alcohol with machines. Of course, in summer it was customary for farmers to supply their labourers with beer, the only safe, cool drink available. Each man would consume an average of six pints a day in very hot weather. Again, in Horringer, in 1837, an inquest was held into the death of one Alfred Last who 'while superintending the work of a threshing machine became later in the afternoon intoxicated, his foot placed incautiously among the wheels of the machine and received several fractures of the leg'.

The introduction of the threshing machine had been the last straw for farmhands, on top of poor living conditions, low wages, a series of poor harvests and a severe winter. In 1830 and 1831, many labourers in Suffolk took part in the notorious Swing Riots, aimed at improving conditions by force, wrecking farm machinery and destroying agricultural buildings. Such actions did not, of course, escape punishment. Those caught and convicted were often sentenced to transportation to Australia.

The prospects for Suffolk farming finally improved in the 1850s. New investment was sunk into buildings, machinery, drainage and other improvements, and profits rose in response to greater demand from a soaring British population. This boom, however, did not last very long. In 1879 there was a disastrous corn harvest following a summer of continuous rain. Cheaper American grain began to flood the market and corn prices plummeted, hitting Suffolk farmers particularly badly. This 'great depression' lasted well into the twentieth century.

CRIME AND PUNISHMENT

Life in Suffolk for the farm worker was undoubtedly tough and with much of the agricultural work being seasonal, families often resorted to stealing. Local newspapers from this time are simply littered with reports of trials of individuals for stealing food, livestock and clothing; in fact, anything they could either consume themselves or sell on to get some money to feed their family. Punishments handed down to petty criminals were severe by modern standards, many receiving prison terms including hard labour for stealing. Hard labour in prison might mean quarrying or building roads. Those who escaped hard labour might be sentenced to solitary confinement.

One of the most common local crimes in rural parts in the Victorian era was poaching. East Anglia was home to numerous country houses owned by the rich who liked to indulge in gentlemanly sports such as hunting and shooting. As a result, many country estates had thousands of rabbits, hares and game birds that proved a great temptation to working-class families eager to feed their children. Landowners employed a number of gamekeepers who, apart from being charged with managing the stock of animals and birds on the estate, also patrolled the grounds around the clock, looking for poachers.

Nineteenth-century prisons were not designed to offer a pleasant experience for inmates. Nevertheless, they were meticulously planned to allow good management of the various categories of prisoner. One of the largest jails in Suffolk was in Bury St Edmunds, which was first occupied by inmates in December 1805. The governor's house had an octagonal plan with alternating long and short faces. In each wall there were windows to oversee the yards around the house. There were four detached wings radiating from the house and each was divided longitudinally to allow two categories of inmate to be accommodated. One half of one of the wings was further subdivided to house both female felons and female debtors. Later two smaller blocks to hold female convicts and juvenile offenders were added. The prison's façade, one of the only remaining pieces of the building, had a flat platform over the doorway that was used for public executions.

Prison was clearly a harsh regime that no doubt became harder with the introduction of the treadmill. This was installed in the mill house in Bury Gaol in 1821 intended for grinding corn and making flour. It was the

Saxtead Green post mill.

invention of the engineer Sir William Cubitt, who was employed by Ransomes iron-founding firm in Ipswich. Cubitt was commissioned by local magistrates to devise a deterrent in an effort to reduce serious crime in Suffolk. What he came up with was a huge revolving cylinder made from iron and wood, with steps like the slats of a paddle wheel. Up to twenty-four men at a time were put to work stepping from one slat to the next. It was described by critics as 'the most tiresome, distressing, exemplary punishment that has ever been contrived by human ingenuity'.

A LANDSCAPE DOMINATED BY SAILS

The landscape of Suffolk in the Victorian era was dominated by windmills. Early in the nineteenth century, almost 500 windmills were at work, most grinding corn. Some were newly constructed, and some were older structures that had been rebuilt. Today only around twenty remain and another seventy partially survive. The earliest type of mills in Suffolk – in the twelfth and thirteenth centuries – were post mills, which were the most popular through the Victorian era in this county, and one of the finest surviving examples is at Saxtead Green near Framlingham. This structure dates back to at least 1796, although manorial records record a windmill in Saxtead since 1287. The post mill is a three-storey roundhouse with four sails carried on a cast-iron windshaft and it has a fantail that, when it is orientated parallel to the wind, means that the main sails are in a position to gain maximum power from the wind. Another type of windmill to be found in abundance in Suffolk was the tower mill and one of the still-functioning mills of this kind is at Bardwell near Ixworth. It was built in 1823 as a four-storey tower with a cap and fantail, like the post mill. It worked by wind until 1925, when an oil engine was fitted that operated for another fifteen years. The mill has now been restored to its former glory by volunteers. Finally, there was the smock mill, which had a timber-framed tower. They are thought to have been invented by the Dutch in the late sixteenth century and brought over to the region mainly to be used to drive scoop-wheels to help drain the fens rather than to drive millstones to grind corn. Crowfield windmill is a surviving smock mill that began life near Great Yarmouth as a drainage mill. In the 1840s, however, it was moved to Crowfield and converted to a corn mill.

In the mid-nineteenth century windmills began a slow decline in the face of competition from large steam-driven flour mills and smaller mills on farms powered by steam or internal combustion engines. Many windmills, therefore, were abandoned, left to become derelict and subsequently demolished.

THE STATE OF RELIGION

The 1851 Religious Census was a unique survey of all identified places of religious worship then in existence, including nonconformist and Catholic chapels, Jewish synagogues, as well as all Church of England churches. This provides an invaluable snapshot of religious practice in Suffolk in the middle of the nineteenth century. More than half of the total 895 places of worship in Suffolk were Church of England (Anglican),

163 Methodist, ninety-one Baptist and ninety independent, along with thirty-one others. The census revealed around 40 per cent of the county's population attended some sort of religious service on one specific afternoon in March 1851. Of these, around 63 per cent of attenders were Anglican and the vast majority of the others were nonconformist.

Although the Church of England attracted more worshippers than all other denominations put together, it had fallen on hard times in the early 1800s. Some churches offered no residence for their minister and nearly a fifth of parsonages were unfit for habitation. However, Ecclesiastical Commissioners, formed in 1836, worked with bishops to introduce reforms and to improve the standard of accommodation for their clergy. The churches themselves were also transformed, influenced by the Oxford Movement. Their renewed emphasis on choir and altar led to drastic restyling, and even rebuilding, of nearly all Suffolk's parish churches. These Victorian restorations of the interiors left many churches hardly recognisable from their former, medieval state. Two of the churches left largely untouched are Badley and Brent Eleigh.

Today we wring our hands with frustration at most of the county's Victorian parish church refurbishments. However, a few surprise and delight such as Huntingfield church. Here, the original medieval ceiling is a painted masterpiece in brilliant colours, with carved and coloured angels, banners, crowns and shields. It was the work of Mildred Holland, the wife of the Rector of Huntingfield. The church was closed for eight months from September 1859 to April 1860 while she painted the chancel roof. Three years later Holland began to paint the hammerbeam nave roof and in September 1866 this was completed. The whole project was a labour of love, inspired by her husband's devotion to the neo-medieval practices of the Oxford Movement. The result is stunning.

EDUCATION FOR ALL

At the beginning of the nineteenth century, fewer than 5 per cent of Suffolk children had access to free education. At this time, small day and boarding schools prolifer-ated in every village and town in the country. They were often run by middle-class, educated men and women who employed visiting tutors for subjects such as dancing and music. These schools, however, were for those whose fam-ilies could afford to pay for an education.

The Church of England, along with other religious denominations in this country, had been a major player in educational provision to working-class children from the seventeenth century. In the 1700s, donations to char-ity schools were commonplace and Sunday schools were found in almost every village community in Suffolk. But it was not until the early nineteenth century that there was a more organised, national approach to such educa-tion. Foremost in this new movement was the British and Foreign School Society, set up in 1808 to support nonconformist educational establishments. The National Society, founded in 1811 as the National Society for Promoting the Education of the Poor in the Principles of the Established Church in England and Wales, fol-lowed suit. It drew on the huge financial resources of the Church of England and was therefore able to spearhead the building of 'National Schools', particularly in rural areas of the county. Although central government grants were available to would-be school boards from 1833 onwards, matching funding had to be found locally or from a society. Despite this challenge, Suffolk witnessed a huge wave of parishes building a new school designed to allow access to elementary education to all children in their community. Many of these Victorian village school buildings in the county, constructed from brick and flint, remain as testament to the commitment of residents to ensure that even children from the labouring class received an education.

As with a number of other Suffolk National Schools, the main driving force behind the new school in Rickinghall, which opened in 1854, was most likely to have been the rector, who had arrived in the village in 1850. Individual subscriptions from residents towards the building of the new school ranged from £80 given by the rector and £30 by the Lord of the Manor, to £1 given by several local tradesmen. Less well-off residents also contributed to the general fund. The total sum required was some £650. Rev. Maul also generously undertook to give over part of his glebe land for the new school site. The building plans followed a standard design for such Victorian schools, which comprised a main schoolroom, a smaller infants' classroom, two porches (one for girls and the other for boys) and two yards (again, one for each sex).

In the thirty or so years following the 'Forster' Education Act of 1870, compulsory attendance at school to a certain age was gradually increased, so that by 1899, all children were expected to attend school until they reached the age of 13. Further schools were built in areas that did not have enough places for the number of children in the community. Thus, by the end of the Victorian era, elementary education was available to all, irrespective of class. As a testament to this achievement, in 1845, just over 50 per cent of Suffolk's population was literate but in 1900 the figure had soared to around 97 per cent.

SELF-IMPROVEMENT FOR ADULTS

In the mid-nineteenth century, a new institution began to appear in villages across Suffolk. Reading rooms were originally imposed upon the working classes by the upper classes, mainly the church and local landowners. Their establishment reflected contemporary attitudes to philanthropy, recreation and self-help, and only served to confirm the great class divide. These reading rooms offered a much-needed alternative to the public house for the working classes, although they tended to appeal more to the lower middle classes. Many, if not all, reading rooms had an emphasis on education and self-improvement through the provision of books and newspapers for the users to read. Other activities, though, were also undertaken, although these varied from village to village. These involved games including bagatelle and draughts, and competitions were frequently arranged with neighbouring village reading-room members.

In 1875, the Suffolk Village Club and Reading Room Association was founded with the instigator of the association, Sir Edward Kerrison, as president. Vice presidents included the Duke of Grafton, the Marquess of Bristol and the bishops of Norwich and Ely. The body's main objectives were fairly straightforward and were primarily 'to assist existing clubs and reading rooms and to aid in the formation of new institutions of the kind throughout the county'. They offered to supply member clubs with rules of successful clubs and to facilitate the exchange of books between reading rooms. In 1879, for instance, grants were given to the Aldeburgh Club for furniture, books were purchased for Haughley and Wattisfield and nearly all its member clubs benefitted from loans of books. The association also owned a magic lantern, which it loaned out, thus facilitating this highly popular form of illustrated lecture across the county. It also gave prizes for contests held by member reading rooms, such as essay and letter-writing competitions.

In the twentieth century, as other diversions appeared and the countryside became more democratised, reading rooms gradually declined. They were, however, an important part of village life in the Victorian era and have left interesting evidence of former lifestyles and attitudes.

THE IRON WAY

The railway was relatively late arriving in Suffolk compared with elsewhere in the country. Although the Grand Eastern Counties Railway had been formed in 1836 with the aim of providing a link from London to Norwich and Yarmouth via Colchester, due to opposition from various vested interests the first steam locomotive did not cross into Suffolk until ten years later. The Colchester–Ipswich line was opened on 11 June 1846 and the day declared a holiday, with the first train arriving in Ipswich to be greeted by 600 ladies waving 'snowy kerchiefs'. In July 1851, Queen Victoria's husband and Consort, Prince Albert, used this new form of transport to visit Ipswich to attend various lectures at the Mechanics Institution and to address a meeting of the British Association for the Advancement of Science. In December 1846 the railway track from Ipswich to Bury St Edmunds was opened, and in November 1849 the main line was further extended from Haughley Junction to Norwich. Ten years later, a major route was completed that connected Ipswich with Lowestoft, via towns such as Woodbridge, Halesworth and Beccles. A number of small train companies ran various different branch lines until the Great Eastern Railway was formed in 1862, amalgamating many of these.

The rail network transformed the wider rural landscape by changing agricultural practices. Farming intensified as expanding railway links ensured that farmers could provide freshly picked fruit and vegetables to London, rather than just for local markets. However, the local newspapers reveal that there were fatal railway accidents, mainly due to people not realising how dangerous and fast was this new mode of transport. Many of the victims were railway workers, such as 50-year-old Allen Gooding, a platelayer with the Great Eastern Railway Company. At an inquest into Gooding's death at Stowmarket station in May 1887, the *Bury and Norwich Post* reported that he was run over by a goods train that was reversing into a siding to get out of the way of a passenger train expected on the platform. Even in the early days of the railway, though, companies offered passengers insurance against death or injury

A bathing machine.

due to a rail accident. For instance, the Rail Passengers Assurance Company advertised in the *Suffolk Chronicle* of 1854 that it would cost £3 10*s* to insure against death for five years. The pay-out to the next of kin would be £1,000.

OH, I DO LIKE TO BE BESIDE THE SEASIDE

We owe our love of the seaside to the Victorians. During the nineteenth century, middle-class family holidays and works outings to Suffolk seaside resorts such as Aldeburgh, Southwold, Felixstowe and Lowestoft were all the rage. This trend was fuelled by three main factors. The first was that medical wisdom started to advocate 'taking the cure' at a spa or coastal town with plenty of fresh sea air. It was also, though, the rapid expansion in the railway network that allowed inner-city residents to access the seaside. And lastly, spending power among the professional classes was such that families could afford to take a break away from the routine of daily life. The working class, too, could benefit from day trips organised by Sunday schools and employers. They embraced a whole host of seaside entertainments such as music hall, brass bands, pleasure gardens and exhibitions.

Aldeburgh was one of Suffolk's earliest seaside resorts. At the beginning of the nineteenth century visitors began to visit the town to enjoy its clear and healthy air and to sample the excellence of its water. A guide book to the town dated 1820 assures its readers that Aldeburgh 'is reckoned by physicians to be one of the most healthy places along the eastern shore, and as remarkable for repeated instances of longevity'. As well as grand hotels, there were fifteen lodging houses and about fifty houses that were 'wholly or in part appropriated for the accommodation of strangers'. The owners of these houses charged seven shillings per week for a room.

In the 1860s, Felixstowe was still a small fishing village. The coming of the railway to the town in the next decade, however, transformed it into a fashionable holiday resort. A further boost was given by a visit to the town by the German Imperial family in 1891. Below the long promenade lined with grand houses built by the Victorian landed gentry, were created beautifully landscaped and sumptuously planted gardens. One of the main attractions of Felixstowe was the spa, where high-quality natural spring water could be drunk. One of the earliest municipal facilities provided for the holidaymaker was a shelter set into the cliff. It cost £2,759 to erect in 1899 and contained a tea room and public conveniences.

One major preoccupation with visitors to the British seaside in the nineteenth century was bathing, and the main aid was the bathing machine. Bathing machines were essentially four-wheel carriages that stood on the beaches. Men and women were strictly separated on different parts of the shoreline. The person got into the carriage through a door, which faced inland. They then changed into their swimwear in the bathing machine and exited it through a door in the opposite side, down some steps straight into the sea. Once mixed gender bathing became socially acceptable in the early 1900s, the days of the bathing machine were numbered.

HERRING (AND MACKEREL)

The seas off the Suffolk coast have always offered up a plentiful supply of fish for the county's fishermen. Much of the fishing until the nineteenth century had been local fleets of small boats, based in the various coastal villages and towns, and launched off the beaches. In the 1800s, however, larger vessels were built, better suited to deep-sea drifting and trawling, aided after the Napoleonic Wars by the decline of Dutch fishing in the North Sea. There was also an increasing demand for cheap food in the rapidly growing industrial towns in the Midlands, and the arrival of the railways made it easier to get fresh fish to consumers across the country. This all signalled a boom in mackerel and herring fishing, in particular, which was to continue through until the outbreak of the First World War. The number of local drifters increased from eighty in 1841 to nearly 400 by 1900. Trawling for fish on the sea bottom, which was developed towards the end of the nineteenth century, saw the numbers of trawlers operating out of Suffolk's main port, Lowestoft, increase from just eight in 1863 to nearly 300 in the 1880s.

In 1844, Southwold was also a thriving sea port with a large fishing station. Local schoolmaster James Maggs kept a diary of all manner of events in the town between 1818 and 1876 and this gives us a fascinating insight into the herring industry. Even with an abundant supply of fish, a large catch was remarkable enough for Maggs to record in his diary on 20 October 1850 that:

> This morning and until about 11 o'clock strong wind from the N.E. About 11 the wind abated when a large shoal of herrings were observed in the bay. Boats and nets were immediately in request and I witnessed that in the course of 4 or 5 hours £100's worth of herring were landed. There would have been more had the boats been larger, as the nets so soon as cast into the sea sank with the quantity of fish.

As the Suffolk fishing industry expanded, men were attracted from farming communities inland to boost the workers from coastal villages. Fishing off the East Anglian coast took place between September and December, which coincided with the slack agricultural period. Therefore, after the harvest was brought in, farm labourers sought work aboard the drifters.

Outside this 'home fishing' season, Suffolk drifters travelled all around the British Isles fishing for mackerel and herring.

From the 1890s onwards, the Suffolk fleet was joined by a large number of Scottish boats during the home fishing season. These Scots brought girls with them to work onshore, gutting and packing the herring. The fish not sold to British markets were cured in brine, packed and exported to Europe.

JUBILATE VICTORIAE

In 1887, the nation celebrated Queen Victoria's golden jubilee. Many towns chose to mark the occasion by erecting clocks or clock towers. One of the better known of these in Suffolk remains the most prominent landmark in the town of Newmarket. To commemorate the Queen's golden jubilee, Newmarket townspeople established a fund to build the three-tier clock tower in a Gothic style. Although the structure of the tower was paid for by public subscription, a local racehorse trainer donated the clock, which had been made by Smith of Derby. The tower incorporates drinking fountains at the base of three of the faces, and a weather vane with a rider and racehorse on the top. The second stage has a carved inscription that reads '1837 Jubilate Victoriae 1887. Clock presented by C. Blanton. Erected by voluntary contribution'.

Queen Victoria was the first British monarch to celebrate a diamond jubilee, in 1897, only four years before her death. In 1896, Queen Victoria had surpassed her grandfather, George III, as the longest-reigning monarch and she asked that any special celebrations be delayed until 1897 to coincide with her jubilee. There were, of course, huge local, national and international celebrations, parties, commemorative services and the like. But many communities across the country also decided to mark this moment in history in bricks and mortar and Suffolk has, perhaps, some of the most stunning of such structures. Holy Trinity Church in Long Melford is without doubt one of the finest examples of a medieval church in the country. In 1701, however, a lightning strike damaged the original tower and it was subsequently demolished. The new tower that replaced it, built fifteen years later, was in red brick, later covered in cement. By the late nineteenth century some of the cement had broken away and the rather ugly appearance of the tower was not considered appropriate for such a grand church. So, as part of Queen Victoria's diamond jubilee celebrations, Long Melford villagers set up a committee to raise funds for a new tower. It took some years to ensure all the funding was in place, but the resulting neo-Gothic design matches the old style of the main church. The new tower was dedicated by the Bishop in 1903. The pinnacles of the old, brick tower had been removed and new, grander pinnacles were named Victoria, Edward, Alexandra and Martyn in honour of the (then) late Queen and the new royal family.

In Bury St Edmunds, the parishioners of St Mary's also put grand plans in place. Apparently spurred on by jealousy – St James' parish already had an illuminated clock face on Moyse's Hall – they raised the necessary funds to put a similar and bigger one on the tower of St Mary's church. The parish magazine for December 1897 carries this rather proud statement:

> The placing of this Clock in the Tower of our noble Parish Church marks – as far as Bury St Edmunds is concerned – the conclusion of events. This great Clock in St Mary's Tower is the permanent memorial in this town of the 60th year of the reign of our beloved Queen Victoria. It is the gift of rich and poor alike.

8

TWENTIETH-CENTURY
SUFFOLK

The life of Suffolk people in the twentieth century was dominated by war, just as it was for the rest of the country. The First World War left no community in Suffolk untouched, not least because of the devastating loss of life of soldiers, sailors and airmen from an entire generation. Suffolk on the home front was also a very different place, with women and boys taking over much of the agricultural labour. Recovery, therefore, in the inter-war period was slow and steady, but the way of life had changed forever. Then the Second World War saw Suffolk play a pivotal role by playing host to American allies in the forefront of the battle in the skies. After the Second World War, Suffolk started slowly to recover. Both agriculture and industry found a firmer footing, and the county gradually grew into the thriving place we know today.

THE GREAT WAR

As soon as the war with Germany was announced in August 1914, mass recruitment was encouraged to bolster the existing regular British army. Some 100,000 men were needed to create a 'New Army'. Recruiting offices were opened across Suffolk in the second week of August. Often these were in private houses of prominent residents in a town or village and many men often had to walk long distances to sign up. Those responding to the call could largely choose their regiment. They were subject to the same physical fitness and age constraints as the regular army. Most signed up for three years or for the duration of the war, bearing in mind, of course, that many thought that the war would be over by Christmas. The war was also greeted with genuine enthusiasm and patriotism, and one recruitment meeting in Southwold in September 1914 produced sixty recruits. Like many other regiments, the Suffolks expanded rapidly from two to twenty-seven battalions. Hundreds of regular and new soldiers did not return from the Western Front, and hundreds more returned wounded. The 7th Battalion was almost completely wiped out at Cambrai in 1917. The 3,000-strong parish of Carlton Colville lost ninety men in the army or navy and another thirty-seven fishermen who were on patrolling and minesweeping duties.

Although an invasion onto the British mainland by German troops was discounted, it was thought that the enemy might try to launch disruptive raids along the coast. Troops were therefore sent to guard likely landing places in Suffolk. In 1916, fears of an invasion were renewed, however, when Lowestoft was bombarded by German ships with the loss of four lives and forty houses. As well as sending heavy arms to the town in response, trenches were dug along the coast, some guns emplaced and concrete pillboxes constructed. More pillboxes were later built south of Lowestoft in 1918. After the war, everything was dismantled apart from the pillboxes. The civilian population started to experience air raids by Zeppelin airships in 1916, and in 1917 Felixstowe was attacked by German seaplanes.

The outbreak of the war did not immediately affect the agricultural communities in Suffolk, as that year's harvest had already been brought in by the time the young men started to sign up at local recruiting offices. However, by 1915 the national agricultural workforce had dropped by 7 per cent and a poor harvest that year meant that County War Agricultural Committees were created to improve the situation. One way in which they tried to boost the local workforce was encouraging women to leave their household duties and to work in the fields instead. However, it soon became clear that work undertaken by women on these agricultural tasks was not sufficient. County Education Committees in Suffolk therefore brought in a system of school exemption certificates to be issued to farmers, who were then allowed to give work to boys over 12 years of age (the normal school leaving age at the time was 14). Later, provision was also made for girls to be exempt from school if they were needed at home to look after their younger siblings while their mothers worked. So, the Great War not only affected the generation of men who fought for their country. The impact on their families left behind was also tremendous, not least on the countless boys and girls who missed out on vital, basic education to keep the economy of their agricultural communities afloat.

TERROR IN THE SKIES

Lying just across from Continental Europe, Suffolk was particularly vulnerable to air attacks by the dreaded Zeppelin. These airships had been designed and developed by Count von Zeppelin in 1900 as a comfortable craft for passenger air travel. Soon afterwards, however, seized on by the German military as potential weapons of war, these 190m-long, hydrogen-filled, rugby ball-shaped balloons soon became objects that struck fear into the British people. They could travel at around 85mph and carry up to 2 tons of bombs.

The first Zeppelin bombing raid over the country was on Great Yarmouth and King's Lynn in Norfolk in January 1915. But it was not long until Suffolk, too, received some devastating blows. Ipswich, Lowestoft and Bury St Edmunds were all bombed in April 1915. Each raid caused considerable damage to both houses and businesses in the town centres, although relatively few casualties were sustained.

Then, on the night of 12 August 1915, Woodbridge was targeted by Zeppelin L10. More than 100 houses were damaged or destroyed and six people lost their lives; a further twenty-three were injured. Those killed included a 17-year-old who delayed leaving his house with the rest of his family when the attack began in order to finish a cup of cocoa; a young married couple, who left behind three children, including an infant only a few weeks old; and a 50-year-old volunteer fireman, killed as he hurried towards the fire station to help the rescue effort. Funerals for the victims took place at Woodbridge Cemetery on 17 August 1915. The whole town closed for business to pay its respects to the victims, and crowds thronged the streets to observe the funeral procession. The 10th London Regiment, which was stationed in the town, provided a military escort, a band, bugles, and a firing party for the burials.

Q-SHIPS

During the First World War, the civilian population in Britain had a role to play, sometimes accidental and sometimes not. It was soon after the start of the conflict, in September 1914, that the Royal Navy sustained its first serious losses of the war: three cruisers were sunk by a German U-boat in the North Sea. Two Lowestoft trawlers – the *Coriander* and the *J.G.C.* – were fishing nearby and the two skippers steered their ships to the battle scene and rescued 156 British sailors from the sea. Their gallantry was honoured in a ceremony at Lowestoft Town Hall a month later, when rewards of £100 in respect of each trawler were presented by the Admiralty and the two skippers were awarded the Board of Trade's silver medals.

The Lowestoft fishing fleet was soon heavily involved in the war at sea. The German U-boats were sinking many of the trawlers. A common tactic was to come alongside, take the catch of fish, order the crew into their lifeboat and then put a bomb aboard the boat.

The war memorial at Bentley.

Therefore, some of the more enterprising Lowestoft skippers persuaded the Admiralty that some of their fishing vessels, called smacks, be secretly armed and operated to decoy enemy submarines. The volunteer crews of these boats – code-named Q-ships – were not to wear uniforms or their gun revealed until the enemy had been lured within range. They were, however, given naval pay as well as danger money in recognition of the peril into which they were putting themselves. When the U-boat was close enough, the cover was whipped off the gun, the Royal Navy's White Ensign was run up the flagpole, and the crew donned naval caps and armbands so that, if they were captured, they might claim Prisoner of War status.

The Lowestoft Q-ships continued to operate successfully throughout the war, the crews receiving many commendations. Once such trawler man was Skipper Thomas Crisp. After a boat that he captained was sunk in August 1915, Crisp was recruited into the Royal Naval Reserve and commanded a Q-ship called the HM Smack *I'll Try*. In July 1917, *I'll Try* was renamed the *Nelson* to maintain its cover following a successful encounter with an enemy submarine. On 15 August, while fishing off the Lincolnshire coast, a German U-boat, *UC63*, was spotted on the surface. The U-boat saw the smack and began firing, scoring several hits before the *Nelson*'s gun was in range. Although hopelessly outgunned, the *Nelson* fought back, but its hull was hit below the water line. A shell hit Crisp, blowing away half his body, but he continued to direct the crew, ordering confidential papers to be thrown overboard and dictating a message to be sent by the boat's carrier pigeons: 'Nelson being attacked by submarine. Skipper killed. Jim Howe Bank. Send assistance at once.' The crew tried to remove their captain from the sinking smack, but he ordered them to throw him overboard rather than slow them down. The crew, however, refused to do so, but were unable to move Crisp and he died in his son's arms a few minutes later. The rest of the crew escaped in the lifeboat and were later found by a search vessel, thanks to their carrier pigeon Red Cock. Crisp was posthumously awarded the Victoria Cross for his bravery and self–sacrifice in the face of this 'unequal struggle'.

REMEMBRANCE

In the years immediately following the First World War, Suffolk communities, along with those across the country, considered how they might best commemorate the great loss of life and sacrifice made by many of their young men. Memorial rolls of honour were put up in factories, sports clubs, railway stations and schools. Church windows were designed and dedicated to military units or individuals. Buildings were constructed to provide 'living memorials', for example as community centres and places for rehabilitation or worship. The Drinkstone War Memorial Institute was opened in the 1920s when the villagers decided they needed a community space for the commemoration of the war dead. Land was purchased in 1921 but they had no funds to pay for the construction of the hall. Instead, a wooden mess hut from nearby Great Ashfield airfield was brought the 6 miles to Drinkstone by horse and cart. It served as the village's community centre until a fire in 2011, when it was replaced.

A great number of towns and villages opted to pay for a stone memorial cross, often with the names of those men who had lost their lives in the war. Across the county, unveiling ceremonies were conducted that gave the communities a focus for their collective grief. A typical village memorial of this sort is at Bentley, which was unveiled on 28 November 1921. The *East Anglian Daily Times* reported that the vicar, supported by a choir, conducted a service for the large crowd. After a brief address, a Union Jack covering the base of the Cross was lifted to reveal the names of the sixteen fallen. The Last Post was sounded and relatives of the fallen placed their wreaths around the foot of the cross.

There were only two Suffolk parishes where every soldier returned alive from the First World War. The term 'Thankful Village' for such communities was first coined in the 1930s. Suffolk's Thankful Villages are Culpho and South Elmham St Michael.

TOWNS VERSUS VILLAGES

At the dawn of the new century, Suffolk was still predominantly a rural county. Only five towns had more than 5,000 inhabitants, their population amounting to only 35 per cent of the county's total. In the first three decades of the twentieth century, Suffolk's population grew by just 8.5 per cent to just over 400,000. Compared with other counties this was a small increase and, in fact, this growth was only in the major towns and their surrounding villages. Ipswich's population increased by more than

The House in the Clouds, Thorpeness.

30 per cent in this time due to its attractiveness to incomers on account of its engineering, brewing and malting industries. Lowestoft grew even more because of its industrial centre and holiday resort status, although this was still overshadowed by Felixstowe, whose population rose nearly 450 per cent from 2,720 in 1901 to 12,067 in 1931. Felixstowe's draw was both because of the tourist industry and as a result of the new port, which was attracting trade from across the globe and expanding exponentially.

Meanwhile, Suffolk's villages, including many former thriving market towns, continued to decline. The exodus fuelled by prolonged agricultural depression that had started in the 1880s continued until the 1930s. Traditional craft trades were also being hit by advances in technology and so millers, wheelwrights, blacksmiths and the like were giving up their trades. There was also a sense of disenchantment with rural life among the younger generations. These people were better educated thanks to the introduction of compulsory education, and a new mobility afforded by the railways, which meant that many country dwellers moved to towns either in Suffolk or further afield. For those who remained, though, village life became more enriched with regular social gatherings, film shows, outings, libraries and reading rooms, as well as a whole host of sporting activities. Although these various initiatives did not halt the decline of rural areas, they certainly improved the quality of life for those who stayed.

After the Second World War, the local population started to grow again strongly and in the 1960s Suffolk's population rose by around 15 per cent, making it one of the fastest-growing parts of Britain. In the main, this increase was as a result of a deliberate policy to attract new residents, and the competition between east and west Suffolk was fierce. Large new estates of both private and council housing were built, and firms and industries were encouraged to move to the county. In west Suffolk, Bury St Edmunds and Haverhill grew by 10,000 residents each and towns such as Brandon, Newmarket, Mildenhall. Sudbury also grew. In the east of the county, Ipswich expanded further, as did Needham Market.

NEVER-NEVER LAND

In 2003, the village of Thorpeness on the Suffolk coast just north of Aldeburgh was voted the weirdest village in

England by *Bizarre* magazine. Although there was originally a small fishing hamlet on this spot called Thorpe,
the village of Thorpeness was created barely a century
ago. In 1910, a Scottish barrister called Glencairn Stuart
Ogilvie bought up the whole area north of Aldeburgh
past Sizewell and inland to Aldringham and Leiston.
Most of the land was used for farming but he was a man
with a dream. That vision was to create a private fantasy
holiday village to which he would invite his friends and
their families. The whole of Thorpeness was designed by
Ogilvie himself, the buildings having a mock Tudor or
Jacobean style. He wanted to recreate the age of 'Merrie
England', which was all the rage in the Edwardian era.
In the centre of the village, and forming a focus for tourist activity today, is a shallow, artificial boating lake that
Ogilvie called the Meare, using the Elizabethan spelling.
Here he built an adventure playground with tiny islands
named after locations found in J.M. Barrie's *Peter Pan*;
the author was a friend. Still in use today, children are
encouraged to land their boats on The Pirate's Lair,
Wendy's House and The Smugglers' Cave, amongst
others. Many of the boats are named after the workmen
who dug the lake.

The other famous feature of Thorpeness is the House
in the Clouds, which was built in 1923 as a water tower.
It was disguised as a house with weatherboarding in
keeping with the rest of the buildings. In 1977 the five-
storey water tower was made redundant when mains
water was supplied to the village, and the structure was
converted into quirky holiday accommodation.

WAR AND THE SPECIAL RELATIONSHIP

During the Second World War, Suffolk residents were inevitably caught up with the national war effort. The county's regiment was once more expanded. Suffolk battalions fought in a number of theatres of war, including at Dunkirk, at the fall of Singapore, in Burma and the D-Day landings in Normandy. It was, though, the war in the skies that changed the Suffolk landscape forever. The county had been used in the First World War as a base for aircraft but except for Martlesham, Felixstowe and Orford Ness, all other military landing grounds had been abandoned after the war. It was not until the 1930s that military aviation was revived in the face of the renewed threat of conflict with Germany. Mildenhall, which opened in October 1934, was the first of four bomber airfields built in Suffolk. The others were Honington, Stradishall and Wattisham. When war was eventually declared, the two civilian airfields at Ipswich and Westley were taken over. Two years into the war, no fewer than twenty-four new airfields were completed or were under construction. When the United States joined the war and wanted to base its enormous offensive air force in Britain, twenty-one sites in Suffolk were identified. Honington and Wattisham were the only two existing airfields used; the rest were new bases that involved bulldozing flat areas of Suffolk's landscape. From these airbases much of the bombing offensive against Germany and occupied Europe took place. From the airfield near Framlingham, for instance, where part of the 8th US Army Air Force was based, 300 missions against the enemy were flown and a total of 19,000 tons of bombs dropped.

After the Dunkirk evacuation in 1940, Britain was on high alert in case of a German invasion and on 7 September 1940 the 'Cromwell' code – which warned of an imminent invasion – was given in error. As a result, there were numerous rumours of landings by sea and German parachutists. It was around this time that stories began to emerge of many badly burnt, dead German troops having been washed up on shores in the south-east, including at Shingle Street, a desolate spot on the Suffolk coast. Like other civilians living along the coastal areas, residents of Shingle Street had already been evacuated because of the threat of invasion. And so, supposedly, there were no non-military eyewitnesses to the incident. However non-official accounts have continued to trickle out ever since. Until all the government files relating to the event are in the public domain, we shall not know the real story, but several theories have emerged as to what happened. It is possible that, indeed, a German invasion force was foiled in its attempt to land on British soil, repelled by flame-throwers, which we know were deployed along the Suffolk coast. Some believe that the bodies were British servicemen killed in a training exercise that went wrong. It may be that the story of dead Germans was all just government propaganda to stir up patriotism, although this does not account for the various civilian sightings of the bodies that have been reported over the years.

THE ENEMY IN OUR MIDST

During the Second World War, around 350,000 enemy prisoners were held in Britain. Suffolk had some prisoner of war camps: at Ellough airfield near Beccles, Flixton airfield near Bungay and at Debach airfield near Woodbridge. There were also numerous temporary camps, often associated with farms or estates, dotted around the county. At first, most of the Suffolk camps held Italians because the authorities were wary of putting Germans here, as they feared the prisoners might gather information on military targets to somehow pass back to their country.

When harvest-time came in 1943 and there was a shortage of labour, volunteers from among the Italian prisoners of war were sought. This was not a great success in some areas and Lord Somerleyton, with others, complained of the Italians' laziness. Despite the complaints, there was no real choice. The labour shortage could not be resolved without employing these prisoners of war. It was not until after D-Day that German prisoners began to replace the Italian workforce. They proved much more popular with the farmers. Although their movement was restricted, the prisoners of war were able to wander around the towns and villages, identifiable by their uniform, often with a big 'P' sewn onto it. Many German prisoners of war remained in Britain for some time after the end of the conflict until the British government was able to repatriate them. It was only in 1946 that restrictions on prisoners associating with the general public were lifted. Until then it had been technically illegal to speak to and to visit a prisoner of war. Despite this, many local residents warmed to their

German guests, treated them kindly and fairly and had a degree of sympathy with their situation. A small number of Germans chose to stay in Suffolk and to make their home there, working on farms as they had done during the war.

LOST FOREVER

Over the centuries, Suffolk's numerous manorial houses and estates have been subject to constant reshaping and rebuilding. Sadly, though, many houses, both grand and small, have been lost, including forty or so that vanished during the twentieth century; some because of fire, although far more through decay and demolition. The reasons were varied and ranged from financial difficulties encountered by the owners to natural threats such as dry or wet rot.

The story of Redgrave Hall is typical of the history and fate of many of these country houses. The Redgrave Park estate, which comprises some 200 acres of land and 50 acres of water, is thought to have been first built on in the thirteenth century. In Tudor times, Sir Nicholas Bacon rebuilt the house and Redgrave Park remained in the Bacon family until 1702, when mounting mortgages forced Sir Robert Bacon, the fifth baronet, to sell. The Redgrave estate remained in the ownership of the Holt and Holt-Wilson family until 1971. Beset by financial difficulties through the second half of the nineteenth century and the first half of the twentieth century, the family eventually sold the now-dilapidated hall for demolition in the 1940s. Originally, the surviving part of Sir Nicholas Bacon's Tudor house was saved in the hope of refurbishing it to provide more modest accommodation. This sadly never happened, and the remains of the house were demolished in 1970.

Other country houses were damaged in the wars. One of these was Rougham Hall, of which only a shell remains. This house was built in the 1820s in a Tudor and Gothic style, replacing an earlier Jacobean manor. During the Second World War, Rougham Hall was used as a base of operations for the armed forces: Rougham airfield was nearby. In September 1940, a stray bomb from a Luftwaffe raid landed in the courtyard, destroying the foundations and causing much of the main building to collapse.

FROM MALTINGS TO MUSIC

Benjamin Britten, a dentist's son from Lowestoft, is one of the county's undoubted stars and he made Suffolk the heart of the twentieth-century British musical landscape. Britten was the first composer to be given a life peerage, and he was also a conductor and pianist. Aside from his musical compositions – including opera, vocal music, orchestral and chamber pieces – he is best remembered for his founding of the annual Aldeburgh Festival in 1948 and the creation of Snape Maltings concert hall. At the festival, Britten and his companion, the tenor Peter Pears, brought together international stars and emerging talent from around the world.

By the 1960s, the Aldeburgh Festival was outgrowing its usual venues in the region and original plans to build a new concert hall in Aldeburgh were not progressing. And so, when redundant Victorian maltings buildings in the village of Snape, 6 miles inland, became available for hire, Britten realised that the largest of them could be converted into a concert hall and opera house. The 832-seat Snape Maltings hall was opened by The Queen at the start of the twentieth Aldeburgh Festival on 2 June 1967 and was immediately hailed as one of the best concert halls in the country. The hall was destroyed by fire in 1969, but Britten was determined that it would be rebuilt in time for the following year's festival, which it was. The Queen again attended the opening performance in 1970. The Maltings gave the festival a venue that could comfortably house large orchestral works and operas, and it continues to host world-class performers under its current management, Aldeburgh Music.

THE COLD WAR

Orford Ness, an 11-mile long coastal strip of shingle beach on the Suffolk coast, played an important role in the Cold War. This eerie, bleak area of marshland was first taken over by the War Department in 1913, drained to form airfields and used by an experimental flying section, which included trials of aerial photography, evaluation of aircraft and the development of camouflage. Prisoners of war were also held in the area to help build the airstrips and the sea defence walls. During the inter-war period, a beacon was constructed to test long-range radio navigation and it was used as a bombing range. Orford Ness was also the site of the first purpose-built experiments during the development of the defence system that would later be known as radar and, having proved the technology, the team moved to nearby Bawdsey Manor and developed the Chain Home radar system in time for its vital role in the Battle of Britain.

Perhaps the part of the site that still holds the most interest and intrigue today are the two 'pagodas' that can be seen from Orford quay. In the 1950s, the Atomic Weapons Research Establishment and the Royal Aircraft Establishment had a base on the Ness, and constructed a number of buildings, including the pagodas, to test nuclear bombs. Whilst no radioactive material was tested on the site, the very-high-explosive initiator charge was present, and the 'pagodas' were designed to absorb any accidental explosion, allowing gases and other material to vent and dissipate in a directed or contained manner. In the event of a

The 'pagodas' at Orford Ness.

larger accident, the roofs were designed to collapse onto the building, sealing it with a lid of concrete and shingle. Later, in the 1960s, an experimental Anglo–American weapons system code-named Cobra Mist was tested at Orford Ness. It involved the detection of aircraft with over-the-horizon radar. This programme closed in 1973 and the site and building were reused as a transmitting station. Until March 2011 the station transmitted the BBC World Service to Continental Europe. Orford Ness is now a nature reserve managed by the National Trust.

FLOOD

As a coastal country, Suffolk residents are aware of the full fury the sea can unleash, and the catastrophic east coast floods of 1953 are still very much fresh in the minds of the many who experienced them. It was one of the worst peacetime disasters ever to hit Britain, striking without warning. Out of the 307 people up and down the east of England who lost their lives as a result of the coastal surge, fifty were in Suffolk; forty-one in Felixstowe alone.

On the night of 31 January 1953, a spring tide combined with gales driving down the North Sea raised the water to a dangerous level. The resulting surge was more than 2½m high at its peak and the sea defences were simply inadequate. In Suffolk there was not a single estuary or valley that was not affected by the flooding, which extended to more than 20,000 acres of land. Trains on the Ipswich to Lowestoft line through Woodbridge were abandoned as the water reached platform level, and a large swathe of the southern part of the town of Felixstowe was flooded. More than fifty beach huts and 100 boats were swept from Felixstowe Ferry on to the RAF base at Bawdsey. Up the coast in Southwold, the town was cut off for two days and part of the South Pier was washed away. Huge trees were uprooted and, inland, whole communities were cut off without power and telephone. Further up the coast at Lowestoft, the sea surge almost immediately engulfed 400 houses. Some lucky residents had been evacuated during the night, and others took refuge on the roofs of their properties.

Many tales of courage and heroism emerged in the immediate aftermath and one of those who received recognition was Leading Fireman John Barley of Lowestoft, who received the British Empire Medal for exceptional bravery when 'without thought for his personal safety he waded neck-deep into the swirling water to save an unconscious man'.

ECONOMIC GROWTH

Economically, life in Suffolk in the early part of the century was dominated by the agricultural depression. Prices were low, the value of land was declining, rents falling and wages rising. The burden on farmers from taxes, rates and tithes was also high. This all led to some farming land being allowed to grass over and buildings being neglected. Nevertheless, there were some enterprising Suffolk farmers who diversified to survive. In Trimley, Clement Smith built a small factory that made cheddar cheese, and Oliver Johnson of Barrow produced vegetables, eggs and poultry for the ever-demanding London market. After a small upturn during the First World War, farms once more became derelict and further previously cultivated land was abandoned in the 1930s. The revival only came with central government's realisation that it needed to protect British agriculture. One of the main Suffolk crops, sugar beet, was subsidised and food marketing boards were established to help farmers reach potential markets. From the Second World War onwards, therefore, Suffolk agriculture gained a firmer footing, and while the number of farms halved, the total acreage of large farms doubled.

During the twentieth century, Suffolk became home to all manner of industry, large and small. Major improvements in the road infrastructure in the second half of the century led to further expansion, especially in the east of the county. The Orwell Bridge has contributed greatly to the ease with which road transport can access the Suffolk coast. Construction of the bridge, started in 1979, was completed in December 1982 and when opened was one of the largest continuous structures in the world. Its main span of 190m runs from the site of the former Ipswich Airport to Wherstead across the Orwell estuary. The bridge carries the A14 to Felixstowe, where the Port of Felixstowe is now the United Kingdom's biggest and busiest container port, dealing with more than 40 per cent of the country's containerised trade. It welcomes more than 3,000 ships each year, including the largest container vessels afloat today due to it having some of the deepest water close to the open sea of any European port. Around thirty shipping lines operate from Felixstowe, offering approximately ninety services to and from some 400 ports around the world. It has

The Orwell Bridge.

its own police, fire and ambulance services. The port is undoubtedly one of the most remarkable success stories the county has to tell.

Some large infrastructure projects in Suffolk, however, have received a less than hearty welcome by residents. The small fishing village of Sizewell was changed forever with the siting of the first nuclear power station in the county. Construction work on the first reactor, Sizewell A, began in 1961 and was officially opened in April 1967. Local opposition to the plan was vociferous, both because of the perceived danger from the power station itself and also from the hazard of transporting the used, irradiated elements by train through the Suffolk countryside to Sellafield in Cumbria. The first reactor was joined by Sizewell B, which was commissioned between 1987 and 1995. It is the country's only commercial pressurised water reactor power station. Sizewell A was then closed in 2006. Plans to build a third reactor at Sizewell are now advanced and seem likely to go ahead.

FREEDOM, NOT LICENCE

In the east Suffolk countryside, not far from Leiston, is a pioneering progressive school. Summerhill was the creation of Alexander Sutherland Neill in 1921 and it runs according to his guiding principle 'Freedom, not Licence'. It is arranged as a democratic community where all aspects of school life are decided by pupils and teachers alike, all of whom have an equal vote at meetings. They are free to do as they choose as long as their actions do not cause harm to others. The important freedom at Summerhill is the right to play. All lessons are optional. There is no pressure to conform to adult ideas of growing up, although the community itself has expectations of reasonable conduct from all individuals. Bullying, vandalism or other anti-social behaviour is dealt with by specially elected ombudsmen or can be brought to the whole community at its regular meetings. After Neill's death in 1973, the school was run by his widow, Ena, and then by his daughter, who is the current principal.

Summerhill became renowned through A.S. Neill's writings and lectures, and many 'copycat' democratic schools have sprung up, especially in the United States. He is recognised as being amongst the top twelve men and women who influenced British schooling in the last millennium. As might be expected, Summerhill has had a difficult relationship with the British government, which regulates and maintains standards of education for all children in the country. This came to a peak in the 1990s when the school was issued with a notice of complaint centred on the school's policy of non-compulsory lessons. After a high-profile court case in 2000, a compromise settlement was reached. The school continues to operate with some seventy-five pupils aged between 5 and 17.

A SECULAR SOCIETY

The Church of England in Suffolk started off on a high note in the twentieth century, with the creation of its own bishopric – the first since the Anglo–Saxon period. In 1914, the diocese of St Edmundsbury and Ipswich was formed with a suitable compromise arrangement between west and east Suffolk: the parish church of St James in Bury St Edmunds was elevated to the status of a cathedral, thus becoming the ecclesiastical seat of the new bishop, but with his residence in Ipswich. However, despite this significant move, church congregations in general – not just Anglicans – slowly began to decline over the century.

In the period between the two wars, Suffolk churchmen bemoaned the indifference of the county's residents to the church's teachings, noting that the younger generation was more interested in cars, motorbikes and cinema. There seemed an even more marked dip in interest in religion later in the century. In 1961, Suffolk had 540 clergy and ministers of religion of all faiths but by 1981 this number had fallen to just 280. Many clergymen were taking on multiple parishes to help the church authorities eke out their meagre funds, and churches were falling into disrepair. The parsonages were becoming too expensive to maintain and many were sold off and more modest accommodation found for the incumbent.

UNITED SUFFOLK

Since 1889, West Suffolk and East Suffolk, together with the county borough of Ipswich, had been three separate administrative entities. No doubt there had been rivalry between the geographic east and west of the county well before this time. However, the new arrangement put in place as part of a nationwide overhaul under the Local Government Act of 1888 formalised the split. This legislation also created county councils, followed in 1894 by a lower hierarchy of district and parish councils. Up to this point, magistrates meeting in quarter sessions – one in the east and another in the west – both administered the county's affairs and meted out justice. Under the new arrangements, administration became the responsibility of the elected local councillors. In the early days of county councils, elections were usually predictable and uncontroversial, with the traditional leaders of society – gentry, clergy and magistrates – being elected. Gradually, however, local businessmen and professionals gained seats. By the outbreak of the Second World War, fourteen women had gained seats on the councils and eventually the mix of councillors showed representatives from almost every walk of life.

It took until 1 April 1974, under the auspices of a further Local Government Act passed in 1972, for the three bodies to merge to form the unified county of Suffolk once again.

9

SUFFOLK TODAY

Suffolk in the twenty-first century is a thriving place in which to live. Visitors, too, flock to the county at all times of the year to soak up the history, heritage, natural beauty and culture Suffolk has to offer.

Suffolk's towns and villages are, arguably, better cared for than in previous centuries. Historic England's listed building status has helped our architectural gems survive and be preserved for future generations. This ensures that all proposed alterations to the fabric of these buildings is considered carefully as part of a formal local planning system. However, even homeowners without such protection are spending time and money restoring houses to their former glory. Good-quality new-builds are using traditional Suffolk building methods such as thatching and pargeting (artwork in plaster on the exterior).

Towns have pedestrianised main shopping thoroughfares and restricted parking. After a trend in the second half of the twentieth century to build large, out-of-town retail centres, the county's towns are encouraging shops back into the centre by offering updated and new facilities. However, both towns and villages are struggling to attract and keep small businesses. Property rental prices have increased and with internet shopping and banking more readily available, this means that fewer residents are venturing out of their houses. Rural post offices are closing at an alarming rate and bus services to and from villages are being cut, thus posing a challenge both for the older generation and for the road transport system.

Ipswich now has a gleaming new waterfront, resplendent with apartments developed from the old warehouse buildings. These stand side-by-side with restaurants, cafés, shops and offices, which all overlook the pleasure craft moored in the marina. The area also now boasts the newly created University of Suffolk. Elsewhere in the town, the public parks are well cared for and provide amenities for young and old. Bury St Edmunds has gone from strength to strength and, although some residents mourned the loss of the old cattle market, the new Arc shopping centre is a bright and vibrant place. After many decades, the cathedral building project is finally finished. In 2005, the skyline of Bury St Edmunds was transformed with the completion of the magnificent Gothic lantern tower. Five years later, an equally impressive painted and gilded vault under the tower was unveiled. Meanwhile, Lowestoft is still working to reinvigorate the town. It now has an award-winning Blue Flag beach with wide golden sands and brightly coloured beach huts. The Victorian seafront gardens are well maintained and provide a welcome oasis in Britain's most easterly town.

The county's churches in the twenty-first century also have a mixed story to tell. At Sunday services, congregation numbers are at an all-time low. Nevertheless, these dedicated few along with their priests, who often juggle a large number of parishes, put time and energy into ensuring that the church buildings are kept in as good order as is possible. This is despite the increasing number of thefts of lead from the roofs. Fund-raising, therefore, has become a regular feature of church life, and bishops are urging them to open up the spaces for local activities. So, in many villages, the parish church has once again become central to the community.

Suffolk's coastline is a main draw for tourists. In the summer months, visitors swarm to our now chic, upmarket seaside resorts such as Aldeburgh and Southwold. The car parks at nearby Walberswick and Dunwich are overflowing with vehicles full of families heading for the beach, followed by fish and chips. The coastal paths and nature reserves are also a major attraction, headed by the world-famous Royal Society for the Protection of Bird's reserve of Minsmere.

The county's architectural heritage is celebrated by residents and visitors alike. The big-ticket properties managed by English Heritage and the National Trust such as Framlingham Castle and Ickworth House attract thousands of tourists each year. Many other privately owned properties are available for us to visit at certain times of the year by appointment, thanks to the 'invitation to view' scheme. Similarly, there are museums large and small in all corners of the county. Christchurch Mansion in Ipswich and Moyse's Hall in Bury St Edmunds are owned and managed by the respective borough councils and give visitors an opportunity to immerse themselves in the history of Suffolk through their exhibits and special events. The Museum of East Anglian Life in Stowmarket presents, in an accessible way, the region's agricultural and industrial heritage.

Culture also plays a large part in twentieth-century Suffolk life. Music and literature festivals abound and The Apex in Bury St Edmunds, an award-winning venue that is home to a diverse programme of live music and events, provides an exciting new alternative to the well-established Snape Maltings. Other towns in Suffolk have created theatres and arts centres from former industrial buildings, such as The Cut in Halesworth, which opened in 2003 in a former maltings. Meanwhile, Newmarket, generally considered to be the birthplace of horseracing, the largest racehorse training centre and the largest racehorse breeding centre in Britain, is home to most major British horseracing institutions and is a key global centre for horse health.

Almost every town and village in the county appears to have benefitted in some way through projects run by volunteers, all intended to preserve and revive interest in local history. From heritage trails and walks to oral history projects aimed at recording the older generation's memories, many of these projects have been made possible through money from the national Heritage Lottery Fund. Other voluntary organisations in the county have taken on larger-scale projects. The Suffolk Mills Group helps care for the county's old windmills and watermills. Some of these newly restored mills are open to the public on certain days in the year, and some once again grind corn to make flour as they had done centuries earlier. The River Gipping Trust is also run by volunteers, who aim to preserve the historic heritage of the river from the centre of Stowmarket to the docks in Ipswich, once an important navigable waterway for the county.

Finally, an initiative to institute an annual Suffolk Day was successfully launched in 2017. Being the sunrise county with Britain's most easterly point, the summer solstice date of 21 June was chosen. It is a day when Suffolk residents can get together and celebrate their history and heritage, arts and culture, innovation and business, as well as the beautiful part of the country in which they live.

SELECT BIBLIOGRAPHY

BOOKS

Bailey, M., *Medieval Suffolk* (The Boydell Press, Woodbridge, 2007).

Blackwood, B.G., *Tudor and Stuart Suffolk* (Carnegie Publishing, Lancaster, 2001).

Champion, M., *Medieval Graffiti: The Lost Voices of England's Churches* (Ebury Press, London, 2015).

De Mille, A.O., *One Man's Dream: The Story behind G. Stuart Ogilvie and the Creation of Thorpeness* (Nostalgia Publications, Dereham, 1996).

Dymond, D., *Parson and People in a Suffolk Village: Richard Cobbold's Wortham, 1824–77* (Wortham Research Group and Suffolk Family History Society, Wortham, 2008).

Dymond, D. and Martin, E., (eds), *An Historical Atlas of Suffolk* 3rd edition, revised and enlarged (The Archaeology Service, Suffolk County Council, Ipswich, 1999).

Dymond, D. and Northeast, P., *A History of Suffolk* revised edition (Phillimore, Chichester, 1995).

Foley, M., *Front-line Suffolk* (Sutton, Stroud, 2007).

MacCulloch, D., *Suffolk and the Tudors* (Clarendon Press, Oxford, 1986).

Meeres, F., *A History of Bury St Edmunds* (Phillimore, Andover, 2002).

Orridge, J., *Description of the Gaol at Bury St Edmunds* (Rodwell & Martin, London, 1819).

Reeve, C., *A Straunge and Terrible Wunder: The Story of the Black Dog of Bungay* (Morrow, Bungay, 1988).

Rimmer, M., *The Angel Roofs of East Anglia* (The Lutterworth Press, Cambridge 2015).

Roberts, W.M., *Lost Country Houses of Suffolk* (The Boydell Press, Woodbridge, 2010).

Rochefoucauld, F.d.l., and Scarfe, N., *A Frenchman's Year in Suffolk, 1784* (Boydell, Woodbridge, 2011).

Scarfe, N., *Suffolk in the Middle Ages* (The Boydell Press, Woodbridge, 1986).

Scarfe, N., *The Suffolk Landscape* revised edition (Alastair Press, Bury St Edmunds, 1987).

Storey, N.R., *The Little Book of Suffolk* (The History Press, Stroud, 2013).

Twinch, C., *The Little Book of Suffolk* (Breedon Books, Derby, 2007).

Twinch, C., *The History of Ipswich* (Breedon Books, Derby, 2008).

Warner, P., *The Origins of Suffolk* (Manchester University Press, Manchester, 1996).

JOURNALS

Proceedings of the Suffolk Institute of Archaeology and History (see www.suffolkinstitute.org.uk)
Suffolk Review: Bulletin of the Suffolk Local History Council (see www.slhc.org.uk)

SUFFOLK PLACE
NAMES INDEX